Doodle-Stitching

Doodle-Stitching

Fresh & Fun Embroidery
for Beginners

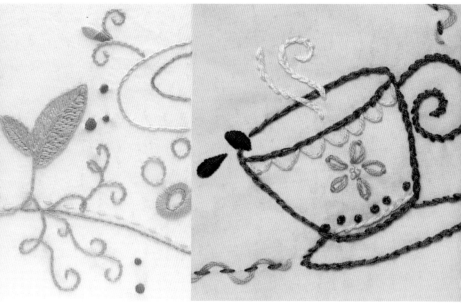

Aimee Ray

LARK BOOKS

A Division of Sterling Publishing Co., Inc.

New York / London

Editor: **Susan Huxley**

Senior Editor: **Suzanne J. E. Tourtillott**

Art Director: **Kathleen J. Holmes**

Cover Designer: **Cindy LaBreacht**

Assistant Editor: **Shannon P. Quinn-Tucker**

Associate Art Director: **Shannon Yokeley**

Assistant Designer: **Travis Medford**

Art Production Assistant: **Jeff Hamilton**

Editorial Assistance: **Delores Gosnell**

Illustrator: **Aimee Ray**

Photographer: **Keith Wright**

Dedication
*For my grandma,
who first showed me how.*

Library of Congress Cataloging-in-Publication Data

Ray, Aimée, 1976-
    Doodle-stitching : fresh & fun embroidery for beginners / Aimée Ray.
    1st ed.
        p. cm.
    Includes bibliographical references and index.
    ISBN-13: 978-1-60059-061-0 (hc-plc with jacket : alk. paper)
    ISBN-10: 1-60059-061-6 (hc-plc with jacket : alk. paper)
    1. Embroidery—Patterns.   I. Title.
TT771.R37 2007
746.44'041—dc22

                                    2007003558

10 9 8 7 6 5 4 3 2 1

First Edition

Published by Lark Books, A Division of Sterling Publishing Co., Inc.
387 Park Avenue South, New York, N.Y. 10016

Text © 2007, Aimee Ray

Photography © 2007, Lark Books

Illustrations © 2007, Aimee Ray

Distributed in Canada by Sterling Publishing, c/o Canadian Manda Group,
165 Dufferin Street, Toronto, Ontario, Canada M6K 3H6

Distributed in the United Kingdom by GMC Distribution Services, Castle Place,
166 High Street, Lewes, East Sussex, England BN7 1XU

Distributed in Australia by Capricorn Link (Australia) Pty Ltd., P.O. Box 704,
Windsor, NSW 2756 Australia

If you have questions or comments about this book, please contact:

Lark Books
67 Broadway
Asheville, NC 28801
(828) 253-0467

Manufactured in China

ISBN 13: 978-1-60059-061-0
ISBN 10: 1-60059-061-6

For information about custom editions, special sales, premium and corporate
purchases, please contact Sterling Special Sales Department at 800-805-5489
or specialsales@sterlingpub.com.

Contents

Embroider Your World

No one knows how long embroidery has been around. For thousands of years people from all over the world have been using colored thread to embellish clothing and household items and to create artwork. While styles change with cultures and years, the techniques are basically the same: passing a needle and thread through fabric. Today, we can use this timeless technique to create fun, fresh, contemporary designs and embellishments.

Embroidery is one of the easiest crafts you can learn. If you're just starting out, there's no need for a huge commitment to buying a bunch of new supplies. The tools are simple and inexpensive; all you really need to get started are a needle, embroidery floss, and some fabric. Learning the basic techniques is simple for someone of any age or experience level. (Thanks to my mom and grandma, I first picked up a needle and thread at about the age of five.)

"Doodle-stitching" is the type of simple embroidery you'll learn in this book. It is also called freeform, or freestyle embroidery. That means there are no rules. You won't have to carefully count your stitches or decipher strange codes. Just thread your needle and start stitching. You'll find lots of whimsical, doodle-style line designs you can use for your embroidery projects, or try your hand at doodling your own. Simply follow a line art design that you've transferred onto your fabric, picking out stitches and colors as you go. You're free to just have fun and be creative!

Embroidery is extremely versatile. You'll find lots of ways to use it in other craft projects or to create a work of art by itself. It can be as simple as a one-stitch decorative edging on a skirt or a tablecloth, or as complex as a full-color picture that you plan to frame and hang on a wall. You can pick and choose your favorite colors and stitches, use an entire pattern or just a small section of it, or combine different elements to custom-design a pattern for your specific project.

Once you learn the basics, you'll also find embroidery to be very relaxing. There's something meditative about filling in a design stitch by stitch and watching it gradually take shape.

Embroidery projects are great to work on while watching a movie on the couch, during long car or plane rides, or just as a way to unwind—wherever you are. Embroidery projects are very portable. Not a lot of preparation is required to get started once you have transferred your pattern to the fabric. Your embroidery also is easily set aside and picked up again whenever you have time to work on it. Whether your day allows you a few free hours, or 10 minutes here and there, you can literally put away your project in mid-stitch and pick it up again later if you need to, right where you left off.

This book will show you, step-by-step, the basic skills you need to start embroidering doodle-stitch style. You'll find lots of fun patterns and project ideas as well. I hope they'll inspire you to pick up a needle and thread and embroider your world.

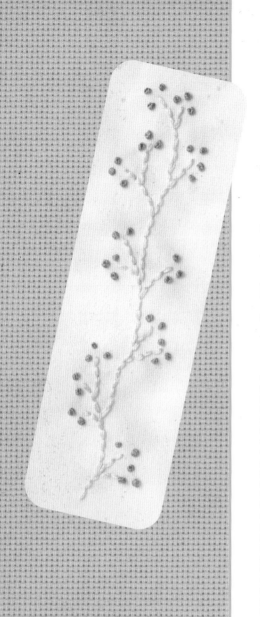

Embroidery Essentials

Embroidery isn't complicated, but knowing a bit about the tools and materials will make your stitching a lot more fun. In this section, you'll learn what to look for and how best to use the items you buy. After you've gathered these essentials and picked your first project, see Getting Started on page 13 for more help. Soon, you'll be turning out great embroidery pieces.

Materials and Tools Checklist

Here's a list of supplies you'll need for almost every project in this book, plus a few extra items that are nice to have on hand.

- 6-inch (15.2 cm) diameter embroidery hoop
- Embroidery and hand-sewing needles
- Embroidery floss
- Fabric stabilizer
- Fine-lead pencil
- Iron
- Nonpermanent fabric marking pen
- Ruler
- Scissors
- Straight pins
- Thimble, leather or rubber
- Tracing and transfer tools
- Tweezers

Materials and Tools

You need to track down a few basic items before you can start embroidering. The materials and tools are relatively inexpensive, and chances are good that you probably have some of them already on hand. If not, you can find them at your local craft store, and they won't empty your piggy bank.

Fabrics

The most common fabrics used for embroidery are quilter's cotton, linen made for handwork, and Aida cloth (a heavy fabric with a large weave). However, almost any fabric is suitable for embroidery. Delicate materials such as chiffon and silk may require an extra bit of care while stretching on a hoop so the weave won't distort or stretch. Also make sure that the stitching isn't so dense that it weighs down—or is visually unbalanced by—a light-weight fabric.

Fine fabrics and stretchy fabrics like cotton T-shirts usually behave better if you apply a removable fabric stabilizer before you start stitching (page 16).

Heavier fabrics such as felt or denim are easy to work with. They don't pucker and may not need to be placed in a hoop (called hooping).

Craft felt is a sturdy fabric. It can handle hand- and machine-stitching and generally won't pucker when embroidered. You don't need to use a hoop with craft felt.

If you're just starting to embroider and need some fabric, take a look at your wardrobe or linen closet. You never know what might inspire you to add a touch of thread to it.

Ready to get started? Embroidery takes just a few simple tools, although you'll probably discover some neat things that you just can't live without.

Cottons, denim/twill, canvas, felt, satin, chiffon, organza, Aida cloth... almost any fabric is suitable for embroidery.

Embroidery Floss

Although you can embroider with just about any thread, the most common is embroidery floss. Each long strand is sold in a small bundle, or skein, and available in any color you can think of. Every color has a number designation, which is printed on the wrapper. Manufacturers, distributors, and stitchers all use the numbers, rather than the names, to identify colors. Some colors are very similar. When you're starting a project, it's a good idea to jot down the numbers you're using in case you need to get more later.

Every floss manufacturer has its own unique set of color numbers. To avoid confusion, the materials and supplies list (What You Need) call for floss by color name. At the end of every project, you'll find a list of the floss brand, color, and color names that were used for the sample shown in the accompanying photo.

If you want to stitch your version of a project with the same colors, but only have access to a different brand of floss, there's an easy solution: Just use the color descriptions in the project's What You Need list as your guide. Or, you can look up the product name and color number on a color conversion chart to find the equivalent number that's available from another company. Almost all specialty shops have a conversion chart to help customers; some retailers sell them, and you can find several free on the Internet by typing "embroidery floss conversion chart" into an Internet search engine.

A length of floss is made up of six smaller strands, or *plies*, that are twisted together. You can use all of them to stitch a thick line, or divide them up and use two, three, or four plies for a thinner line on fine details. The designs in this book are meant to be embroidered with all six plies, unless indicated otherwise. However, if you're embroidering a design at a reduced size, you may want to decrease the number of plies.

There are a variety of specialty threads, such as linen, metallic, silk, and wool, which are also fun to try.

A rainbow of colors and textures are yours to explore when you shop for embroidery floss.

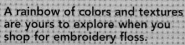

Needles

A good embroidery needle is medium sized, with a sharp point and a long opening, or eye, at one end, which makes threading your floss through it much easier. It's a good idea to have a small-eye needle on hand as well, for sewing fabric by hand with a single ply of floss or sewing thread. Buy a packet with several sizes and types of needles to ensure that you have on hand, whatever size you want to use.

Embroidery Hoops

An embroidery hoop is a two-piece frame. Plastic hoops are sturdier than wood and last a long time. Hoops come in many sizes. A 6-inch (15.2 cm) diameter hoop is good for almost any project; small designs will fit inside the circle and, for larger designs, you can move the hoop around as needed.

Scissors

Keep a pair of small sharp sewing scissors on hand while embroidering. You need them to cut lengths of floss and snip off any leftover floss when you're finished stitching.

Tools for Transferring

To transfer a design—and sometimes a pattern—from this book or from another source to your fabric, start by copying it onto tracing paper, as explained on pages 14 to 15, or by making a photocopy.

The next step is getting the design or pattern onto the fabric. Depending on the fabric and density of the completed stitching, you might be able to trace the lines with a lead pencil or chalk. Otherwise, you can draw on your fabric using a nonpermanent fabric marking pen or pencil that's specially made for this purpose. (The instructions advise when a lead pencil or chalk is suitable.) Nonpermanent fabric marking pens come in several varieties. Some make marks that wash away with water, and others have marks that simply fade over time. If you choose a fabric pen that has disappearing, or air-soluble, ink, be sure it's not for a project that you'll be working on for several days. Your tracing may fade before you're finished.

Don't let the transfer process intimidate you. It's easy, and you can choose a method that's most suitable for you. Options abound: transfer paper, chalk, a nonpermanent tracing pen, or try tracing using a light table.

Dressmaker's carbon paper can be purchased at most craft stores. It comes in several light and dark colors, to suit dark or light fabrics.

Iron-on transfer pencils allow you to trace the design onto tracing paper, and then iron it onto your fabric.

Marks from some transfer tools become permanent when ironed. Test, test, test on a scrap of the project fabric!

Other Useful Tools

Pins and a small pincushion are always good to have around when doing sewing projects.

If you have trouble threading your needle, a needle threader makes the job quick and easy.

You'll be glad to have a thimble on your finger when pushing the needle through tough fabrics like denim or canvas. A leather or rubber thimble will protect your fingers and also help you get a good grip on the needle. Place the thimble on the index or second finger of your dominant hand—whichever one you use to push a needle through any fabric. You also might want to place another thimble on your opposite hand to protect the finger that receives the needle underneath your work.

The more embroidery projects you do, the more floss you'll accumulate. You might find it useful to organize the strands by wrapping each color on a plastic or cardboard holder; write the color number on the holder; and then store them together in a box. Special boxes are sold to contain these, but you can use an ordinary, clear plastic fishing tackle box.

Finally, although the real purpose of pinking shears is to keep fabric edges from fraying, their toothed blades can create decorative edges on appliqué shapes.

Getting Started

Beginning your embroidery project is wonderfully simple. All you need to do is transfer the design, hoop it, thread the needle with embroidery floss, and start stitching. For more tips—and information on a few simple techniques—read on.

Choosing a Design

In Doodle-Stitching you'll find lots of unique designs for you to use for your embroidery projects. You can stitch up these designs according to the project instructions, or mix and match them to create your own compositions.

Using a photocopier, you can even reduce or enlarge these designs so that each one perfectly fits your project. Some of the designs in this book are the right size for the patterns and dimensions in the instructions. When a design (or a pattern) has to be enlarged, there's a note to this effect. You'll see it when you trace or photocopy the book page.

But don't stop here! Almost anything can be used as an embroidery

Grab your hoop, a needle, some floss, and a design . . . these items, plus a few basic tips will get you on your way.

One design, three very different results. Feel free to choose your favorite colors and stitches to make every design uniquely yours.

design. An image with strong outlines and simple details works best. Look at clip art books or Web sites, coloring books or, of course, draw your own. You have an artist inside you, whether you know it or not. Does your drawing ability limit itself to the doodles you make while talking on the phone? Guess what? Those simple little pictures and shapes can become great embroidery designs, as shown in the photo above. Draw large, or enlarge your little doodles on a photocopier. Cut them up and arrange the doodles into an interesting composition. Try overlapping different shapes or adding a decorative border. Words also make great designs. Use your own handwriting, or type them up using your favorite font and use the printout as your design. Transfer your completely original design to fabric, just like you would any other.

Transferring a Design

In order to transfer an embroidery design or pattern to your fabric, you can use one of the methods explained here. In a few projects, a specific method is suggested because it's most successful for the featured fabric. You can use any method you like when none is suggested.

Whatever method you choose, it's important to first preshrink the fabric by washing and drying it the same way that you'll care for the finished piece. Then you should press the fabric because it needs to be wrinkle-free before it's hooped. Since marks from some transfer tools become permanent when ironed, it's best to press your fabric before transferring a design to it.

In every method, you'll first want to either photocopy or trace the designs from the pages of this book.

Light Method

The easiest way to get a design onto a light-color fabric is to trace it, using a light box or a sunny window. Tape the design to the light source, place your fabric over it, and then trace the design with a regular lead pencil or fabric pen.

Carbon Paper Method

Dressmaker's carbon paper in a contrasting color is ideal for dark- or light-color fabric. Spread your fabric on a hard surface and position the design on top, both with the front, or right side, up. Slide a sheet of carbon paper between the layers, transfer side down. Pin or tape the fabric and design together so they don't move while you work, and then trace over the design with a ballpoint pen, pencil, or other blunt tool, like a knitting needle or chopstick. Press hard. The chalky marks from transfer paper sometimes fade as you work. If you notice the design is wearing off, go over the lines with a fabric pen or white chalk.

Transfer Pencil Method

A third way to transfer your design to fabric is to use an iron-on transfer that you make with a special pencil. First, trace the design onto tracing paper using a pencil or fine-tip marker that'll give you dark lines. Flip the paper over and trace your lines again, on the opposite side, with the transfer pencil. Now tape the paper, transfer side down, on the fabric. Press it with a hot iron to transfer the design to the fabric.

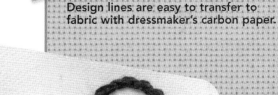

Design lines are easy to transfer to fabric with dressmaker's carbon paper.

15

Adding Fabric Stabilizer

Stretchy, flimsy, and loose-weave fabrics are much easier to embroider if you first apply a fabric stabilizer to the back. A stabilizer keeps fabric from stretching while you work to help make a smooth finished product.

There are many stabilizers, usually identified by the way that they're applied: sprays; liquids; adhesive sheets (press-on or iron-on); and a type that's hooped with the fabric and secured to it as you stitch (sew-on). Stabilizers also are classified by the removal method: tear away, water soluble, or heat soluble (heated with an iron until it crumbles). Some stabilizers are designed to remain on the back of the work. In almost all categories, there are thick and thin versions that are sold as fabric or plastic-like sheets, strips, or rolls. With so many options, you're sure to find a stabilizer that's suitable for your fabric, techniques, and personal preferences.

Whenever a project sample made for Doodle-Stitching needed a stabilizer, a self-adhesive product was used. Look for a thinner, press-on stabilizer intended for machine embroidery because it's easier to stitch through.

To apply the stabilizer, cut a piece slightly larger than the entire design. Iron the fabric to remove wrinkles and then apply the stabilizer to the back of the fabric, or wrong side, according to the instructions on the package.

After embroidering the entire design, you can remove the stabilizer. To remove tear-away stabilizer, carefully pull the paper off the fabric. Rip the stabilizer into smaller pieces, if necessary, to avoid tugging at your stitches. Use tweezers to remove bits of paper caught under the stitches.

Only a few projects in this book call for a type of fabric that needs to be stabilized.

Preparing the Fabric and Floss

Even if you back your fabric with a stabilizer, you still should use a hoop. Only firm fabrics, such as denim and felt, don't need to be hooped.

To make your fabric taut, spread it over the smaller inside hoop and fit the larger (outside) one over the top with your fabric in between. Tighten the little screw that's on the outer hoop and gently pull on all the edges of the fabric until you have a taut surface (figure 1).

Figure 1

The edges of the stabilizer can be caught in the hoop. Next, thread the needle. Start with a length of floss 12 to 18 inches (30.5 to 45.7 cm) long.

Getting all six plies of a strand of embroidery floss through the needle's eye can be a challenge. It may help to slightly dampen your finger and twist the end to a point, or squeeze the floss ends flat between your thumb and forefinger. Slide the needle's eye onto the floss (instead of pushing the floss through the eye). If all else fails, use a needle threader; it'll save you a lot of headaches.

After you've inserted an end of the floss through the needle, knot the longer end. Wrap the floss end around your finger, roll it off, and tighten it (figure 2).

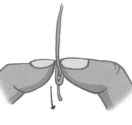

Figure 2

Stitching the Design

You can complete all of the colors and stitch types in a section of the design before moving on. Or, you can work a single color throughout the design, then switch to a new color and work it in the same manner.

Starting at the back of the fabric, pull the needle and floss through until the knot catches. The floss will likely twist up after a while. To correct this problem, hold up the hoop and let the needle and floss hang straight down loose, so that the strand can untwist. Be careful, and don't lose your needle!

When you're down to a 2- or 3-inch (5.1 or 7.6 cm) length of floss on the needle, pull the strand through to the back of the fabric. Pass the needle under a stitch, bring the needle back through the floss loop, and tighten (figure 3). Snip off the loose end near the knot.

Figure 3

Finishing Your Work

You may want to hand-wash the finished piece in cool water with a mild detergent. Gentle laundering removes any unseen oil or dirt that accumulated during handling and any marks from the transfer pencil. Squeeze out the excess water by rolling the work in a towel. Spread your project flat to dry. When it's dry or just slightly damp, place it face-down on a clean terrycloth towel and iron out any wrinkles from the back. Pressing from the back prevents the iron from crushing the embroidery stitches.

Stitch Library

It's time to play! Now that you've gathered your supplies and learned the basic process that's involved in embroidering a motif, you're ready to start stitching.

Embroidery stitches are easy to learn. By mixing and matching a few simple stitches, you can create almost any look that you can dream up. Don't be afraid to experiment. As you embroider more and more, you'll discover techniques best suited to your style. Soon you'll be designing your own projects.

Outline Stitches

Outline Stitches are the base of almost any design. You'll use these to "draw" on the fabric, following the lines of the design, or *design lines*. On their own, outline stitches can be combined to create a graphic image that's full of lush detail, as shown in the piece photographed on page 20. Whenever you make outline stitches, it's most important that the fabric you're working on is taut. These stitches are the foundation of your design, so it's important to start with quality work.

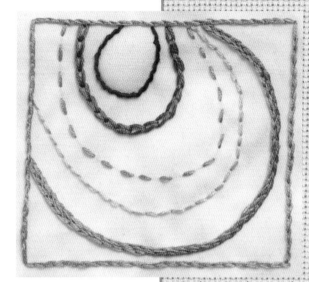

Outline Stitches can be used to trace lines, or arranged in rows for an interesting pattern.

Straight Stitch

Pull the needle and floss to the front of the fabric at A (figure 4). Move the needle forward along the design line, and then return to the back of the fabric at B. The distance from A to B can be as long or short as desired.

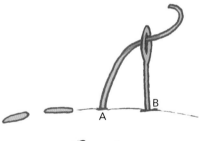

Figure 4

Several Straight Stitches in a row are called *Running Stitches*. They can be worked on a straight or curved design line. Usually, the individual stitches are the same length, and the distance between each stitch is the same.

You can scatter small Straight Stitches for a random pattern, which are called *Seed Stitches* (figure 5). You can make Seed Stitches as long or as short as desired.

Figure 5

A Straight Stitch is as basic as embroidery gets.

Split Stitch

On the front of the fabric, make a small stitch that's twice as long as the desired finished stitch, from A to B (figure 6). Bring the needle up through the center of the stitch, at C, to split the floss in half. Make another long stitch on the surface, and then split it, to continue the line of stitching.

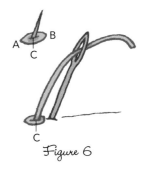

Figure 6

The Split Stitch is great for nice, thick outlines, plus it's easy and quick to make.

Back Stitch

Start with a small stitch in the opposite direction, from A to B (figure 7). Still underneath the fabric, start a "forward" stitch that's twice as long as the first. Bring the needle to the front of the fabric at C. To make each new Back Stitch, once again start by working backward on the surface, inserting the needle at the end of the previous stitch, at A.

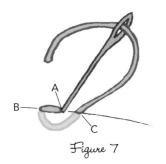

Figure 7

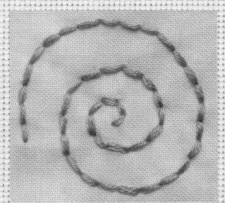

Used alone, the Back Stitch is an attractive design element. It can also give a design a clean outline.

Stem Stitch

Make a stitch, from A to B (figure 8). Leave the floss a little loose. Pull the needle through to the front at the midpoint and just to one side of the previous stitch, at C. Pull the floss tight. Continue this process to make a length of Stem Stitches along the design line.

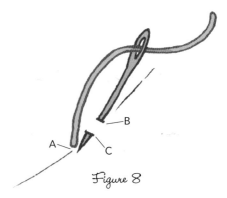

Figure 8

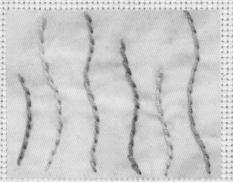

The Stem Stitch works well for curves, which makes it ideal for representing a flower stem.

Figure 9

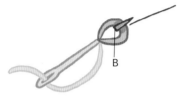

Figure 10

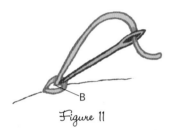

Figure 11

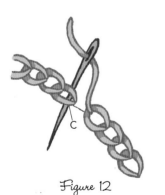

Figure 12

Chain Stitch

Pull the needle and floss to the front of the fabric at A. Insert the needle and floss back into the fabric at A (figure 9). Pull the floss to the back of the fabric until you have a loop about ⅛ inch to ¼ inch (.3 to .6 cm) long. This loop is secured at the same time you start a new one, as follows: Bring the needle and floss to the front of the fabric near the top of—and inside of—the previous loop at B (figure 10). Pull the needle and floss to the underside, still at B, until the new loop is the same length as the previous one (figure 11). Continue making additional loops in the same manner. To secure the last loop in a line of Chain Stitches, bring the needle to the front of the fabric as if you're starting a new loop. Make a tiny stitch over the end of the loop.

Ending a Chain-Stitched circle is slightly different. Work Chain Stitches, as described above, around the circle until you're one stitch shy of the first loop. Pull the needle and floss to the front of the fabric as if you're going to make a new loop. Slide the needle underneath the start of the first stitch, at C, and then insert it back into the fabric at the end of—and inside—the last finished loop (figure 12).

The Chain Stitch is fine for outlining shapes, but it's a little thicker than a Split Stitch and works better for decorative borders.

Practice all of your Decorative Stitches on a single piece of fabric and you'll have a work of art when you're finished.

Decorative Stitches

Your creativity is best expressed by decorative stitches. While there's a specific way to make each one, you get to decide the length and angle that determine the personality. A blanket stitch, for example, can be sharp and modern, or you can make each stitch looser—and space them closer together—for a more romantic effect. As you make the designs in this book, let your style shine through. Some of the described stitches are meant to be worked in a continuous line, while others are made independent of each other.

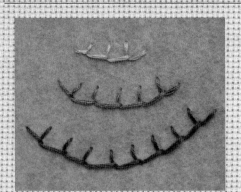

The Blanket Stitch is great as a border or an edging.

Blanket Stitch

Starting on the design line, make a loose diagonal stitch away from the line, from A to B (figure 13). Bring the needle up to the front of the fabric on the design line at C (if working at an edge, you won't stitch over the edge). Catch the first stitch under the needle tip and pull the floss tight to the design line (or fabric edge). Make a new diagonal stitch, on the opposite side of the design line, to start the process again.

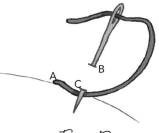

Figure 13

Scallop Stitch

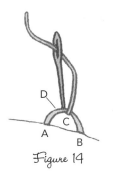

Figure 14

Make a loose stitch on the design line, from A to B (figure 14). Finger-press the stitch flat to one side of the line, so the center of the top is the desired depth of the finished scallop. Bring the needle to the front of the fabric at the center of the previous stitch, at C. Insert the needle on the outside of the loop to hold the top of the scallop in place, at D.

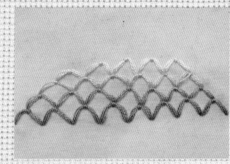

Scallop Stitches have long been favored for borders, but stacking them in rows is a less common treatment.

Threaded Running Stitch

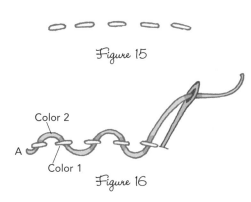

Figure 15

Figure 16

Color 2

Color 1

A

Make a line of small, close Running Stitches (figure 15). End this floss. Start a second floss strand, in another color, at the same spot as the first line of stitches, at A (figure 16). Working only on the front—without stitching through the fabric—insert the needle under the first Running Stitch, then through the second Running Stitch. Continue weaving the second color back and forth under the Running Stitches until the end of the line. End this floss. Weave additional lengths of floss through the straight stitching—on top of the fabric—in any manner, if desired.

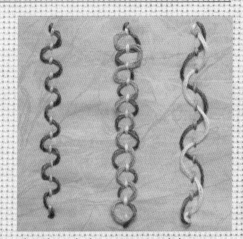

The Threaded Running Stitch has a unique look—especially when worked in several colors and with more than a single line of weaving on the surface.

Cross Stitch

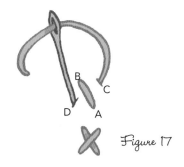

Figure 17

Start with a small diagonal Straight Stitch, from A to B (figure 17). Make a second stitch from C to D. Rows look neater when the lines for each cross (X) overlap in the same direction. Connected Cross Stitches become Herringbone Stitches, as shown in the lowest row of the photo at right.

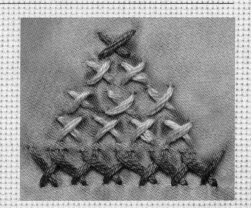

Made much the same way, the finished appearance of a line of Herringbone Stitches takes on a different effect than multiple Cross Stitches, shown on page 25.

The French Knot is a nice accent stitch for making tiny dots. You also can use it to fill an entire area with an interesting texture.

Herringbone Stitch

Decide the height of the finished stitch. Draw a parallel line this distance from the design line. Starting on the design line, make a loose diagonal stitch to the next line, from A to B (figure 18). Make a short horizontal stitch on the back of the fabric by bringing the needle to the front at C. For the downward diagonal stroke, insert the needle on the design line, at D.

For a line of Herringbone Stitches, as shown in the photo at left, top, for each stitch, bring the needle to the front of the fabric slightly to the left of the last position, and make a new diagonal stitch between the design and parallel lines.

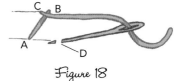

Figure 18

French Knot Stitch

Bring the needle and floss to the front of the fabric at A (figure 19). Wrap the floss around the base of the needle in the direction shown. Place the needle back into the fabric close to the previous position, at B (figure 20). Pull the floss tight and close to the fabric as you pull the needle through to the back of the fabric.

Most of the French knots used in this book's designs are made by wrapping the floss around the needle once. A label on the design will tell you if more than one wrap is needed.

Figure 19

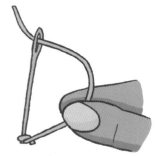

Figure 20

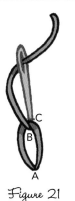

Figure 21

Lazy Daisy Stitch

Make a small loop by pulling the needle and floss to the front of the fabric at A, and then returning to the back of the fabric at A (figure 20). Finger-press the loop flat. Anchor the top of the loop to the fabric with a small stitch, from B to C. A Lazy Daisy Stitch can be a single petal, as explained above. For a daisy, make additional loops, always starting in the center, at A.

The Lazy Daisy Stitch is used to make flower petals or leaves. Use Satin Stitches or French Knots to define the flower centers.

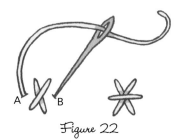

Figure 22

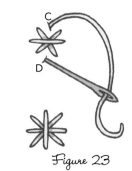

Figure 23

Star Stitches

Start a Cross Stitch Star by making a Cross Stitch (page 25). Now make a Straight Stitch (page 21) on top, from A to B (figure 21).

Start an Eight-Point Star by making a Cross Stitch Star. Now make one more Straight Stitch on top, from C to D (figure 22).

Start a Center Point Star with a Straight Stitch (page 21) that begins at the center, at A, and goes in any direction, to B (figure 23). Again bring the needle out at A, this time going down in a different position, at C. Make as many stitches as desired, all the same length, beginning at A, and ending in a previously unstitched spot.

Stars can be stitched in several different ways. French Knots are scattered as accents.

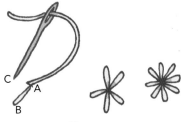

Figure 24

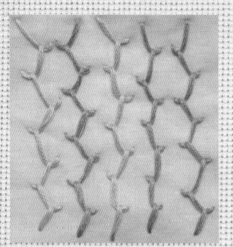

This stitch works well for imitating decorative foliage and plant shapes.

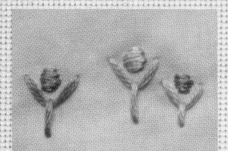

Like the Feather Stitch, the Fly Stitch is unique and makes good foliage. Use a different stitch for the flower heads.

Feather Stitch

Starting on the design line, make a loose diagonal stitch away from the line, from A to B (figure 25). Beside B, bring the needle to the front of the fabric on the design line, at C. As you pull the needle through at C, catch the previous diagonal stitch under the tip of the needle. Make another diagonal stitch in the opposite direction, to D (figure 26).

For a line of feather stitching, bring every loose diagonal stitch back to the design line by catching it under the needle tip, and alternating the direction of the diagonal stitches.

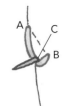

Figure 25

Figure 26

Fly Stitch

Make a loose horizontal stitch, from A to B (figure 27). Finger-press the stitch flat to one side. Bring the needle to the front of the fabric at the center of the previous stitch, at C. Make a second, longer, stitch perpendicular to the first by inserting the needle at D, thus trapping the center of the previous stitch.

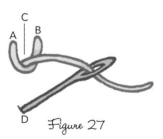

Figure 27

Fill Stitches

The Satin Stitch and the Long and Short Stitch are two of the more common ways to fill spaces. You also can use Straight Stitches (page 21), French Knots (page 26), or Cross Stitches (page 25) to fill larger areas of your embroidery with interesting textures.

Solid areas of color are eye-catching in embroidery pieces.

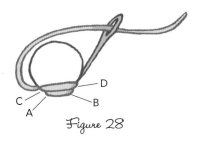

Figure 28

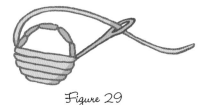

Figure 29

Satin Stitch

Make a Straight Stitch from one design line to another, from A to B (figure 28). Make a second Straight Stitch (page 21) close to the first, again going from a design line to the opposite one, from C to D. The stitches might not be the same length, but it's more important that every stitch starts and ends on opposing design lines. Continue making additional stitches in the same manner, positioning each one close to the next so that the fabric underneath isn't visible.

If you have trouble keeping the design edges even, first outline the area with tight Back Stitches (page 22) or Split Stitches (page 22), and then making Satin Stitches on top of the Outline Stitches (figure 29).

The Satin Stitch will give a beautiful, smooth finish to solid areas of your design. It's best to use the Satin Stitch only for small spaces. Since the stitches are long and sit on top of the fabric, they can sometimes get snagged.

The Long and Short Stitch is used to cover large areas with a solid or blended field of color.

Long and Short Stitch

The name Long and Short Stitch is misleading, because only the first row has different stitch lengths.

Start Row 1 with a long stitch, beginning on the design line and extending into the area you want to fill, from A to B (figure 30). Don't try to make the stitch reach the opposite design line. Bring the needle and floss to the front of the fabric at the design line, beside the previous stitch, at C. Go down at D, so the new stitch is parallel to the first but only half as long. Make another long stitch, then a short one, and so on to the end of the row. Don't work the first row around a curve. Instead, start a second row, as explained below, so every row is straight.

In all of the following rows, the stitches are all one length. Start the second row by making a stitch above the last one of the first row, from E to F (figure31). The next stitch is the same length, worked above the second last stitch of row 1, from G to H. The row 2 stitches appear to be different heights because they're stacked above a long or short stitch. In the same manner, continue stacking new, same-length stitches on top of the ones below, adding more rows as needed to fill the space.

You can create a *blend* between light and dark colors by stitching a

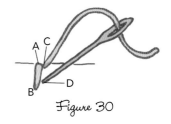

Figure 30

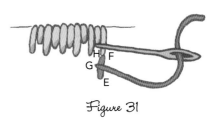

Figure 31

few rows in a light color, and then the next few in a darker shade, and so on. Don't worry too much about keeping the length of your stitches exactly uniform and, as you fill in your shape, you'll probably need to add an extra stitch here and there to fill in spaces as needed. Just try to keep all your stitches going in the same direction, and you'll have an evenly filled area when you're finished.

Sewing Essentials

Don't worry—the projects in this book involve very little sewing. But you do need to learn some very simple techniques so that you can showcase your beautiful embroidery on a finished project.

Appliqué

Stitching a piece of contrasting colored or patterned fabric onto a fabric surface adds more depth to embroidery. Can you imagine, for example, how boring the Nightingale Lap Quilt (page 92) would be without the circles?

Felt is great for appliqués. It's thick, easy to cut, and doesn't fray. You just cut out the finished shape, and sew it to the background fabric.

When using cotton or other fabric, you can cut the appliqué edges with pinking shears to give them a decorative look and reduce fraying.

Felt and pinked appliqués are attached to the background fabric with outline or decorative embroidery stitches (pages 24 to 28), appliqué stitches (figure 32), or hidden stitches (page 33).

One of the more traditional ways to make an appliqué yields a clean, folded edge. Start by drawing a shape on the appliqué fabric. Now cut it out ¼ inch (.6 cm) beyond the outer lines of the shape. Press the ¼-inch (.6 cm) seam allowance to the back of the appliqué shape. You can attach this shape to the background with appliqué stitches (figure 32).

Appliqué Stitch

Place the appliqué on the background fabric. Pull a knotted length of floss or sewing thread from the underside of the background fabric to the front at A, which is very near—and through—the edge of the appliqué (figure 32). Still on the front of the work, insert the needle through only the background fabric at B, to make a tiny stitch perpendicular to the edge of the appliqué. Don't pull the needle through to the back of the fabric. Instead, start the next stitch by inserting the needle tip at C. Continue making even-length, equally spaced stitches around the perimeter of the appliqué.

Fabric appliqué is an interesting technique often used with embroidery.

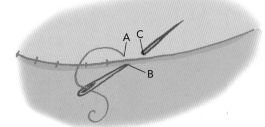

Figure 32

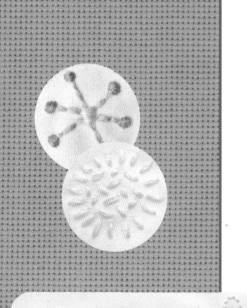

Embroidering with Beads

There's no end to the number of effects that are possible by adding beads to embroidery.

The process isn't tricky as long as you use a needle that's suitable for the bead. The size of the holes in different beads will vary, so check that your embroidery needle can be pulled through the hole. If it can't, pick up a package of beading needles. These are long skinny needles with tiny eyes. Available in a range of sizes, they're designed to pass through the hole of even the tiniest bead.

After threading the needle with matching sewing thread or one or more plies of embroidery floss, again pass the needle through a bead to make sure that the floss isn't too thick for the hole. If it is, switch to a same-size bead with a larger hole, or get slightly larger beads.

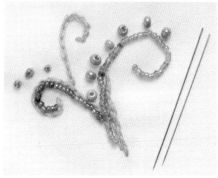

Beads add sparkly accents to your embroidery.

Pony beads are large enough for you to pull yarn through, and they're usually plastic. You don't need a special needle to thread these. Seed beads are glass or plastic. Your local craft shop might sell these tiny beads in several sizes, all of which are small enough to sit on the tip of a slightly long fingernail. Pick whatever seed bead size you like, because any will look great worked into the designs in this book.

Beads can be stitched to fabric one at a time, using a Straight Stitch (page 21) or a Back Stitch (page 22). With the needle and floss on the front of the fabric, just slide the bead onto the needle, snug it up against the fabric, and complete the stitch in the usual manner.

Double Hem

Your projects will look neat and professional with this hem. You just fold under the fabric edge twice, and then stitch it in place. Every project that calls for a double hem will tell you the desired finished width.

Here's the process for making a ½-inch (1.3 cm) double hem:

Along the cut, or raw, fabric edge, fold ½ inch (1.3 cm) to the underside. Press the fold. You now have a flattened fold at the edge. Turn this under, to the back of the fabric, so that the new fold is ½-inch (1.3 cm) wide (figure 33). Sew a line of Straight Stitches along the top of the innermost fold, through all of the fabric layers.

Figure 33

Hidden Stitch

This is an invisible stitch used to close holes in pillows or toy animals after they're stuffed.

Use sewing thread that's the same color as the fabric. You'll be working from the outside, or *right side*, of the piece. Fold under the excess fabric (the seam allowances) along each side of the opening. Butt the folded edges together.

Thread a needle with matching sewing thread with a knot at the end. From the back of the fabric, insert the needle through one of the folded edges so the knot is trapped in the fold and the thread is on the outside of the fabric at a folded edge, at A (figure 34).

Pull the needle and thread through the folded edge at B, directly across from A. Slide along the inside of the fold and pull the needle to the outside at C. This traps the stitch inside the fold. Insert the needle through the opposite fold, at D, which is directly across from C.

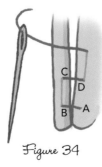

Figure 34

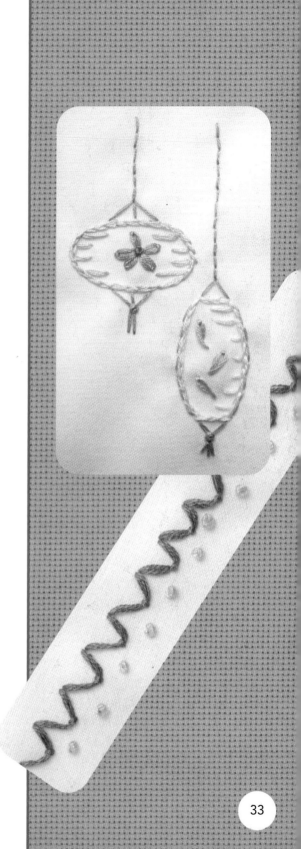

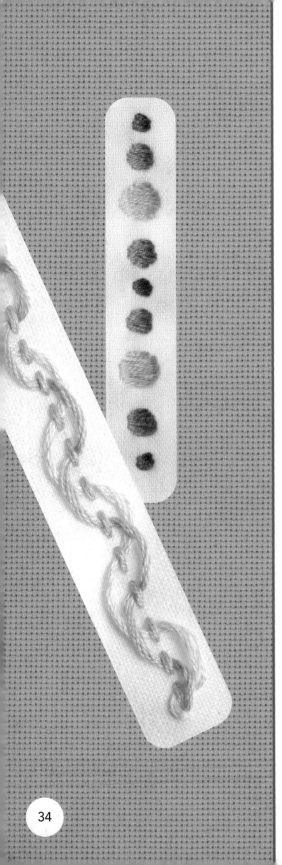

Tug on the thread to pull the two sides of the fabric together. Continue sewing back and forth, trapping the stitches inside the folded edges. Keep your stitches small and close together and you'll barely see them when you're finished. End the thread with a tiny knot buried in the underside of one of the folds.

Topstitch

Topstitching is worked after fabric pieces are sewn together, and the project is turned right side out. You work by hand or by machine.

Just sew a line of small Straight Stitches (page 21). Keep the stitches close together, evenly spaced, and all the same length. The stitches are usually placed close to—and parallel with—an edge, but they can be made anywhere.

Whip Stitch

This is a great way to add a decorative touch while joining pieces of fabric along matched edges. You can use it to sew together two edges by stitching loosely and then opening the pieces flat when the seam is complete. For extra punch, use contrasting floss rather than sewing thread.

Starting at the back—or between two pieces of fabric—bring your needle and floss through to the front at A (figure 35). Bring the needle over both layers, at the edge. From the outside of the bottom fabric layer, insert the needle through both fabrics, at B. Continue stitching along the matched edges, making every diagonal stitch the same length and the same distance apart.

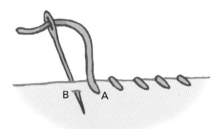

Figure 35

Projects

There are hundreds of ways to stitch embroidery into your daily life. As you start to embroider, you'll find more and more ways to use your work and surround yourself with unique, personalized items that express your creativity. Here are some fun and easy projects to get you started.

Sewing Circle Bag

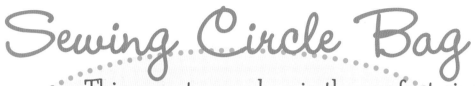

This easy-to-sew bag is the perfect size and shape to hold a 6-inch (15.2 cm) embroidery hoop and materials.

What You Need

2 pieces of tan twill fabric, 12 inches square (30.5 cm)

Geometry compass

Nonpermanent fabric marking pen

Sampler design

Embroidery floss, 1 skein each of blue and light blue*

12 inches (30.5 cm) of blue grosgrain ribbon, 2 inches (5.1 cm) wide

The author used DMC embroidery floss in colors 3755 and 3753.

Stitches

All

Finished Size

10 inches (25.4 cm) in diameter.

Instructions

1 Line up both squares of fabric with the wrong sides out. Using the geometry compass, mark a 10-inch (25.4 cm) diameter circle with a fabric pen. Leaving ½ inch (1.3 cm) of extra fabric outside the traced line, cut out the circle through both layers of fabric.

2 With the circles still together, find a point near the top that measures 7 inches (17.8 cm) across, from one drawn line to the opposite drawn line. With the fabric pen, draw a line straight across, and mark an X on each side, directly on the line for the circle. This is for the opening at the top of the bag.

3 Transfer the Sampler design to the front of the bag and embroider it.

Sampler design

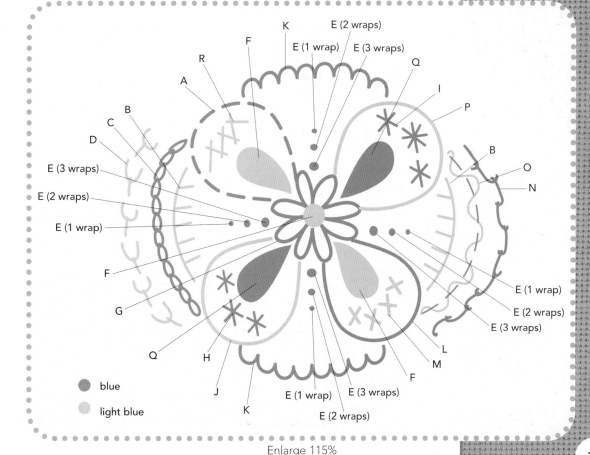

Key
A Straight Stitch
B Blanket Stitch
C Chain Stitch
D Fly Stitch
E French Knot
F Satin Stitch
G Lazy Daisy Stitch
H Center Point Star
I Cross Stitch Star
J Stem Stitch
K Scallop Stitch
L Split Stitch
M Cross Stitch
N Feather Stitch
O Threaded Running Stitch
P Back Stitch
Q Long and Short Stitch
R Herringbone Stitch

● blue
● light blue

Enlarge 115%

4 Line up the two circles with the wrong sides out. Fold the ribbon in half along the length, just at the ends. Tuck the ribbon between the two fabric circles and pin the ends in between the two layers of fabric just below the X marks (figure 1).

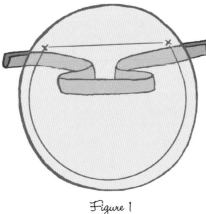

Figure 1

5 Using the Back Stitch, or a sewing machine stitch, sew around the circle, leaving the top (between the X marks) open.

6 Cut small notches in the fabric around the edge, up to—but not through—the seamline (figure 2). This will help smooth the edges.

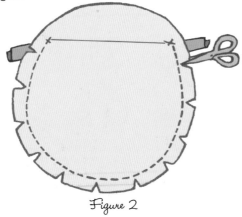

Figure 2

7 Turn the bag right side out and fold the top (loose) edges at the opening to the inside, along the straight line that you drew (figure 3). Press the sides flat.

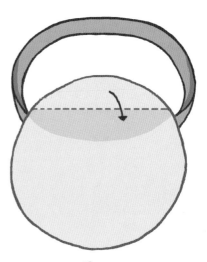

Figure 3

8 Using the darker blue embroidery floss and the Whip Stitch, sew along the top edge of the opening. When you're finished, snip off the extra fabric flaps on the inside, 1 inch (2.5 cm) from the top. Now you have a handy reference to all the embroidery stitches in this book right at your fingertips.

All-Seasons Ornaments

Crayon tinting adds extra color to these ornaments. There's one for each of the four seasons.

What You Need

8-inch square (20.3 cm) of white cotton fabric

Four Seasons designs (pages 40 and 41)

Wax crayons, 1 each of green, light green, light blue, light orange, red orange, light pink, salmon, and yellow

2 pieces of paper, 8½ x 11 inches (8.5 x 27.9 cm)

Embroidery floss, 1 skein each of bright orange, dark orange, medium orange, coral, coral red, light coral, light yellow, medium blue, pale green, and white*

4 plain or patterned cotton fabric circles, 3¼ inches (8.3 cm) in diameter

20 inches (50.8 cm) of white ribbon, ⅛ inch (3 mm) wide

Pony beads, 4 each of blue, green, orange, and red

White sewing thread

Polyester fiberfill

Pinking shears

The author used DMC embroidery floss in colors 349, 352, 353, 445, 722, white, 800, 3348, 3853, and 3854.

Stitches

French Knot

Split Stitch

Straight Stitch

Finished Size

2¾ inches (7 cm) in diameter.

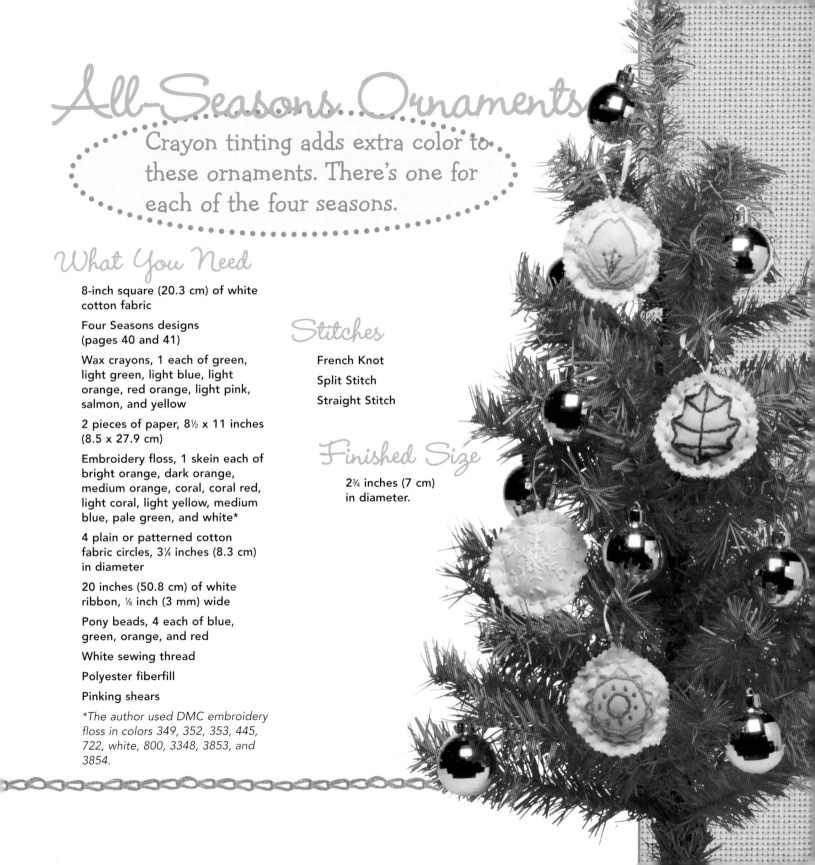

Instructions

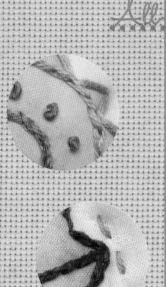

1 Transfer the Four Seasons designs to the front of the white fabric. Leave ½ inch (1.3 cm) of extra fabric around each circle, for seam allowances. Don't cut out the circles yet.

2 Place the fabric with the circles on a soft surface, such as a piece of fabric folded into several layers. Working on the right side of the fabric, lightly color inside each circle with the crayons. Use more than one color to blend an area from light to dark. Use light orange and yellow for the sun; green, light green, light pink, and salmon for the flower; and light orange and red orange for the leaf. The fabric for the snowflake design has only one color, light blue, which fades out from the center. Leave the central star of the snowflake white. Don't press too hard. You can add more color after step 3, if you want darker motifs.

3 Place the colored fabric between the pieces of paper and press with a very hot iron. This sets the color. Any extra wax from the crayons will bleed into the paper. If you want the color to be darker, lightly color over the areas again when the fabric has cooled, and then press again.

4 Embroider the designs. Don't embroider the outer circles yet.

Four Seasons designs

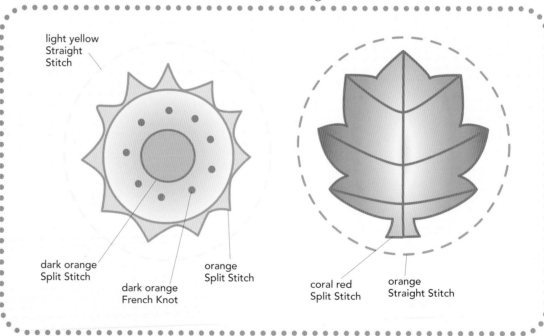

light yellow
Straight
Stitch

dark orange
Split Stitch

dark orange
French Knot

orange
Split Stitch

coral red
Split Stitch

orange
Straight Stitch

5 Using pinking shears, cut out each circle ½ inch (1.3 cm) away from the outermost circular design line for each ornament.

6 Cut out a circle of the same size from patterned or colored fabric for the back of each ornament.

7 Cut a 5-inch (12.7 cm) length of ribbon for each ornament. Pull each length of ribbon through four beads. Using white sewing thread, sew both ends of a ribbon to the top of each ornament, on the back of the white fabric.

8 Line up a patterned or color fabric circle against each embroidered

circle with right sides facing out. Pin together each pair.

9 Using Straight Stitches and the color noted on each design, join the back and front of a pair by sewing three-quarters of the way around, ½ inch (1.3 cm) from the matched edges. Don't end the stitching. Tuck a small amount of polyester fiberfill inside and then finish sewing the circles together. You can start and end your floss with knots, hiding them between the two layers of fabric so that they don't show.

Four Seasons designs

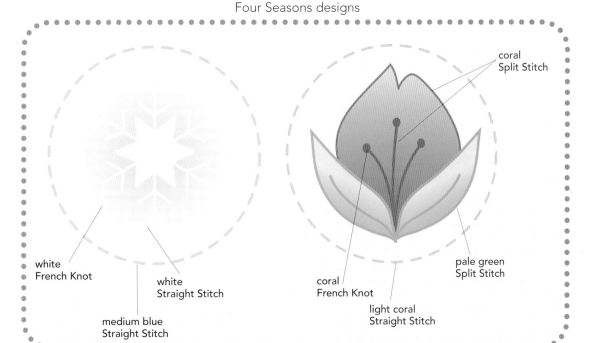

white
French Knot

white
Straight Stitch

medium blue
Straight Stitch

coral
French Knot

light coral
Straight Stitch

pale green
Split Stitch

coral
Split Stitch

Felt Forest Creatures

Stuffed animals are sure to bring smiles to faces of all ages.

Stitches

Back Stitch (optional)

French Knot

Straight Stitch

Satin Stitch

Split Stitch

What You Need

Owl design (page 44)

Raccoon design (page 44)

Blue transfer paper

6 sheets of felt, 9 x 12 inches (22.9 x 30.5 cm): 2 tan, 2 brown, 1 cream, and 1 dark brown

Embroidery floss, 1 skein each of aqua, turquoise, brown, dark chocolate brown, coral, black, and white*

Sewing thread, cream and dark brown

Polyester fiberfill

Pointed tool like a knitting needle or pencil

The author used DMC embroidery floss in colors 310, 352, 420, 598, 807, 838, and white.

Finished Sizes

Owl: 4¾ x 5¾ inches (12 x 14.6 cm); Raccoon: 9 x 6½ inches (22.9 x 16.5 cm)

Instructions

Note: Instead of buying different colors of sewing thread for each appliqué fabric, separate a piece of matching embroidery floss and use one of the six plies.

1 Using blue transfer paper, transfer the Owl design (page 44) to the tan felt and the Raccoon design to the brown felt. Center the designs so that you have at least 1 inch (2.5 cm) of fabric all the way around them. Don't cut these out yet.

2 Stitch the outline of each animal on the marked felt, using the specified floss color and the Split Stitch. You don't need to use a hoop with craft felt.

3 Photocopy or trace the appliqué shapes that are marked on the Owl and Raccoon designs. Transfer the Owl shape and Raccoon belly to the cream felt and the Raccoon tail, and eye shapes to the dark brown felt. Trace the eyes and color decorations on these pieces as well. Cut out the appliqué shapes.

4 Pin the appliqué shapes in place on each animal. Using the matching sewing thread and needle, hand-stitch around the edges—through both the appliqué and animal shape layers—with Straight Stitches. Keep the stitches small so you'll barely see them when you're finished.

5 Embroider the shapes following the color, stitch, and lines on the designs and appliqués.

6 Line up the second pieces of tan and brown felt with the corresponding embroidered fronts and pin them together. Leaving a 1 inch (2.5 cm) border of fabric beyond the stitched outlines, cut out each animal shape through both layers of the felt.

7 Remove the pins, flip over each piece, and line them up again so that the stitched front faces inward (wrong side out.) Pin the pieces together.

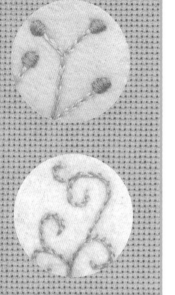

8 Sew around the outside of each animal with sewing thread, ½ inch (1.3 cm) from the edges, through all of the felt layers. Leave a 2-inch (5.1 or 7.6 cm) long opening at the bottom.

9 Carefully snip notches ½ inch (1.3 cm) apart around the edges—up to but not through the stitching. The curved areas need to be trimmed the most: Make the snips even closer together at these locations. Snip off the extra felt from any pointed areas, such as the ears. Trimming the fabric beyond the stitching will help the seamline look smooth.

10 Turn each animal right side out through the opening.

11 Stuff both of the animals. Make sure that you push enough polyester fiberfill into the tight corners. A pointed tool such as a knitting needle or pencil can help you do this. When an animal is full, fold in the edges around the opening and close it using the Hidden Stitch. To hang your animals on the wall, stitch a small loop of floss to the back of each one.

Racoon and Owl designs

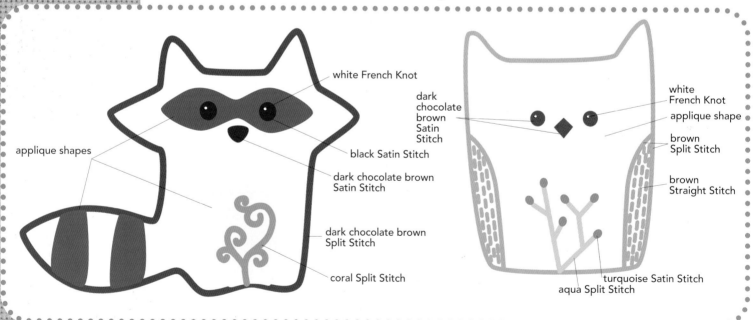

Enlarge 240%

Enlarge 224%

Songbird Wristlet

Keep music at your fingertips with this wristlet made for an MP3 player.

What You Need

Singing Bird design and Songbird Wristlet pattern (page 47)

9 x 12 inches (22.9 x 30.5 cm) aqua or light blue fabric

Embroidery floss, 1 skein of black*

Sewing thread to match fabric

8 inches (20.3 cm) of black ribbon, ½ inch (1.3 cm) wide

½-inch (1.3 cm) circle of hook-and-loop tape

The author used DMC embroidery floss in color 310.

Stitches

Lazy Daisy Stitch

Satin Stitch

Stem Stitch

Straight Stitch

Finished Size

¾ x 2½ x 4 inches (1.9 x 6.4 x 10.2 cm).

Drawstring style

Flap style

Songbird Wristlet

Instructions

Note: The following instructions make a holder with a flap top. To create a draw-string holder, before cutting the fabric alter the Songbird Wristlet pattern. Follow steps 1 to 3. Continue with step 4, making a ½ inch (1.3 cm) opening at each corner, along the long edges and starting ¾ inch (1.9 cm) from the end. Turn the piece right side out. Don't sew the openings shut at any point. Topstitch along both short ends and again 1 inch (2.5 cm) from the top edge. Continue with steps 7 to 10, ignoring the ribbon references. Draw the ribbon through the openings and sew the ends together.

1 Fold the fabric in half. Trace the Songbird Wristlet pattern onto the top layer of the fabric. Mark the pattern fold lines.

2 Cut the pattern shape from both layers of fabric. Set aside one of the fabric pieces for use in a later step, as the lining.

3 Copy the Singing Bird design to the front of the remaining fabric shape. Embroider it, using three plies of floss for all of the stitching.

4 Place the front of the lining against the front of the embroidered pieces. Match all of the cut edges. Join the fabric pieces by sewing around the perimeter ¼ inch (6 mm) from all of the edges, leaving a 2-inch (5.1 cm) opening along one edge (figure 1).

5 Turn the joined pieces right side out. Sew the opening closed with the Hidden Stitch (page 33). Press the seams flat.

6 The rounded end will be the flap that covers the top opening of the finished wristlet. Topstitch along the rounded end. Topstitch along the opposite short end (figure 2).

Figure 1

Figure 2

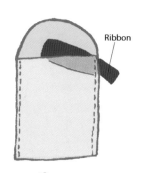

Ribbon

Figure 3

Figure 4

7 Fold the short end of the joined piece along fold line A, with the embroidered design on the inside and the lining on the outside. Match the short end to fold line B.

8 Bring together the ends of the ribbon to make a loop. Tuck the ribbon inside the folded wristlet, just below fold line B. Let the ribbon ends extend beyond the edges at one side. Sew the layers together along each side, catching the ribbon ends in the stitching at the top of one side (figure 3).

9 With the lining still on the outside, pull the front away from the back at one

bottom corner to make a triangle that has the bottom seam on one side and the side seam on the opposite side of the same corner. Pinch this corner flat. Sew a line straight across it, ¼ inch (6 mm) from the point (figure 4). Stitch the remaining bottom corner the same way.

10 Turn the pouch right side out. For the closure, sew or press the hook-and-loop tape to the center of the flap and a corresponding position on the front.

Singing Bird design and Songbird Wristlet pattern

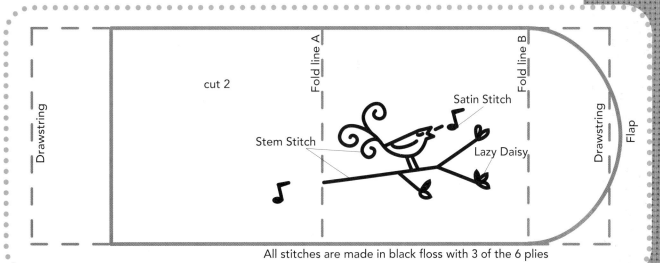

Drawstring · cut 2 · Fold line A · Satin Stitch · Stem Stitch · Lazy Daisy · Fold line B · Drawstring · Flap

All stitches are made in black floss with 3 of the 6 plies

Enlarge 200%

Spring Leaves Wall Art

A canvas frame is a great way to
display your embroidered artwork.

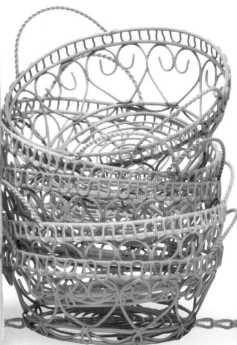

What You Need

Pollination design (page 51)

16-inch square (40.6 cm) of white cotton fabric

Embroidery floss, 1 skein each of coral, dark coral, light coral, light brown, pale green, and yellow green*

4-piece wood frame for 8-inch square (20.3 cm) canvas

8-inch square (20.3 cm) of mat board

Stapler

The author used DMC embroidery floss in colors 165, 351, 352, 353, 422, and 3348.

Stitches

Lazy Daisy Stitch

Long and Short Stitch

Straight Stitch

Satin Stitch

Split Stitch

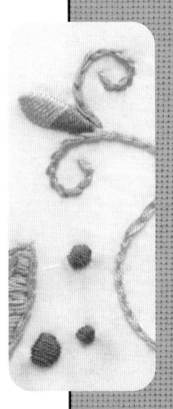

Finished Size

8 inches square (20.3 cm).

Instructions

1 Transfer the Pollination design to the fabric, leaving a 4-inch (10.2 cm) border of fabric around the design.

2 Embroider the design.

3 Fit the four canvas frame pieces together. Spread the embroidered fabric face down and center the mat board on top of it. Center the frame on top of the mat board.

4 Make sure that the front of the fabric is smooth and the embroidery is centered. Wrap and staple the excess fabric to the back of the frame, starting with the top and bottom (figure 1). Attach the sides next (figure 2).

5 Fold the corners, as shown in figure 3. Staple them down.

6 Add more staples around the frame, 1 inch (2.5 cm) apart, pulling the fabric tight as you go.

7 Trim off the extra fabric on the back. Sign and date your masterpiece on the mat board.

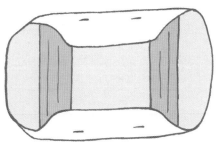

Figure 1

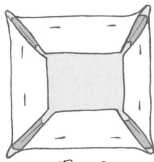

Figure 2

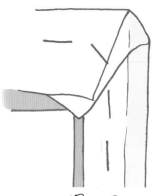

Figure 3

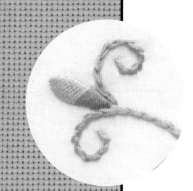

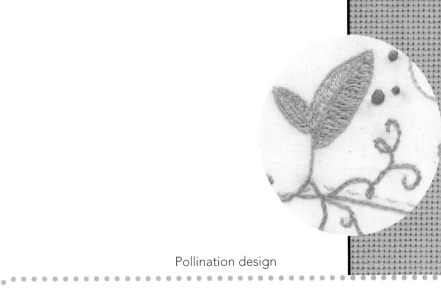

Pollination design

Key

A coral Satin Stitch
B coral Split Stitch
C dark coral Satin Stitch
D light coral Straight Stitch
E light coral Split Stitch
F light coral Satin Stitch
G light brown Split Stitch
H light brown Satin Stitch
I pale green Long and Short Stitch
J pale green Satin Stitch
K pale green Split Stitch
L yellow green Long and Short Stitch
M yellow green Split Stitch
N yellow green Lazy Daisy Stitch

Enlarge 180%

Fire and Ice Butterfly Patches

Bright butterfly patches will add flair to your favorite threads.

What You Need

Red Butterfly and Blue Butterfly designs

9 x 12 inches (22.9 x 30.5 cm) of white craft felt

Embroidery floss, 1 skein each of coral red, coral, dark coral, light coral, and metallic copper for the Red Butterfly design; 1 skein each of aqua, light aqua, dark periwinkle, periwinkle, light blue, medium blue, and metallic silver for the Blue Butterfly design*

Seed beads, 5 red for the Red Butterfly design; 4 aqua and 6 dark blue for the Blue Butterfly design

Beading needle

Light blue and red sewing thread, or an 8-inch square (20.3 cm) of fusible webbing, for attaching the finished patches

*The author used DMC embroidery floss in colors 340, 341, 349, 351, 352, 353, 598, 747, 800, 3753; Light Effects (Jewel) E168 and E301.

Stitches

Long and Short Stitch

Satin Stitch

Split Stitch

Straight Stitch

Whip Stitch

Finished Size

Red Butterfly Patch: 3 x 3½ inches (7.6 x 8.9 cm); Blue Butterfly Patch: 4 inches square (10.2 x 10.2 cm).

Instructions

1 Transfer the butterfly designs to the felt.

2 Embroider the design, starting with the Split Stitch for the outline. You don't need to use a hoop with craft felt. Stitch the body and spots next, followed by filling in the open spaces with Long and Short Stitches. When working the wings, blend the floss colors (page 30). Add the beads last (for beading guidance, see page 32).

Red Butterfly and Blue Butterfly designs

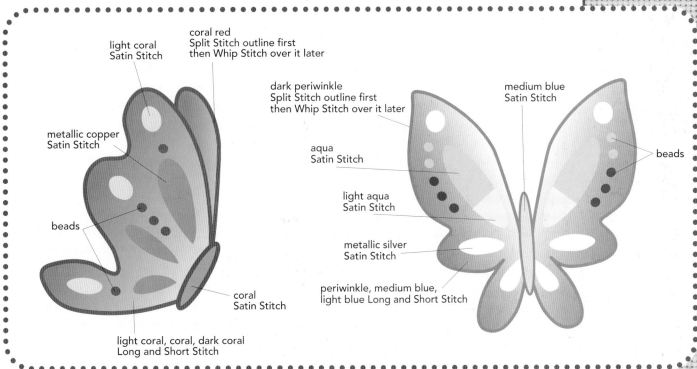

light coral
Satin Stitch

coral red
Split Stitch outline first
then Whip Stitch over it later

metallic copper
Satin Stitch

dark periwinkle
Split Stitch outline first
then Whip Stitch over it later

medium blue
Satin Stitch

aqua
Satin Stitch

beads

light aqua
Satin Stitch

beads

metallic silver
Satin Stitch

coral
Satin Stitch

periwinkle, medium blue,
light blue Long and Short Stitch

light coral, coral, dark coral
Long and Short Stitch

Enlarge 156%

3   Cut out the butterfly shapes very close to the perimeter of the Outline Stitches. Make sure you don't accidentally snip through any of your embroidered stitches.

4   Using the Whip Stitch, sew around the edge of each butterfly, covering the Outline Stitches (figure 1). This will hide the raw edges of the felt and give your patches a nice finished edge.

5   Sew the patches onto any fabric surface with tiny Straight Stitches along the edges, just inside the border. If desired, you can iron on the patches with fusible webbing. Felt can get fuzzy when laundered too much. To protect your patches, wash the patched garment in cold water and let it air-dry.

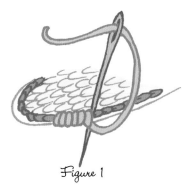

Figure 1

Bohemian...Tunic

Forget transferring the pattern!
Build this border as you stitch.

What You Need

Decorative Edging design
(page 57)

Linen tunic

Embroidery floss, 4 skeins each
of dark turquoise and turquoise*

Beading needle

Seed beads, 3 dark turquoise
and 6 turquoise for every pattern repeat

*The author used DMC embroi-
dery floss in colors 807 and 3809.*

Stitches

Chain Stitch

French Knot

Lazy Daisy Stitch

Satin Stitch

Scallop Stitch

Split Stitch

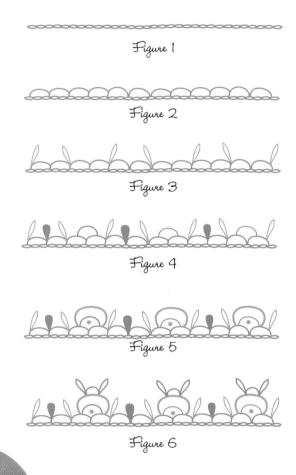

Figure 1

Figure 2

Figure 3

Figure 4

Figure 5

Figure 6

Instructions

Notes: The size and style of your tunic will affect the amount of floss that you need. If in doubt, buy additional floss. You may need a small embroidery hoop to fit into the sleeves. Check the sleeve opening before you buy a hoop.

1 You'll probably find it easier to work freehand, following the step-by-step instructions and figures. You can, however, copy and then transfer the Decorative Edging design to the tunic. Since the necklines and sleeves are round, the end of the design will meet at the place you started. The design probably won't match up perfectly at the beginning and end, so start at a seamline so that any small discrepancies are less noticeable. Keep your stitches at each step as uniform as you can.

2 Using dark turquoise embroidery floss, make a line of Chain Stitches close to the edge (figure 1). The tunic shown on page 55 has a border seam 1½ inches (3.8 cm) from the edge. This was a natural place to position the first line of embroidery. If your tunic doesn't have a border seam, you can start stitching on the edge, or a short distance from the edge all the way around the neckline and sleeves.

3 Make Scallop Stitches above the Chain Stitches (figure 2).

4 Switch to turquoise floss and make a Lazy Daisy Stitch at the end of every second Scallop Stitch (figure 3).

Decorative Edging design

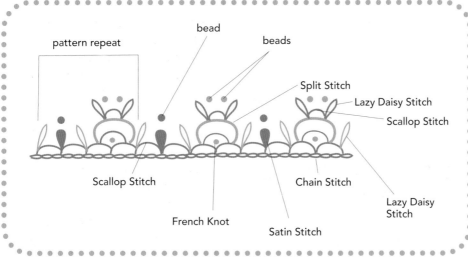

pattern repeat · bead · beads · Split Stitch · Lazy Daisy Stitch · Scallop Stitch · Scallop Stitch · Chain Stitch · Lazy Daisy Stitch · French Knot · Satin Stitch

Enlarge 159%

5 Using dark turquoise floss, Satin Stitch inverted teardrops and more Scallop Stitches, as shown in figure 4.

6 With turquoise floss, center a French Knot in—and make a Split Stitch loop above—each scallop you made in the last step (figure 5).

7 Add a Lazy Daisy Stitch and a Scallop Stitch, both worked in dark turquoise floss, to the top of the stack you built in the last two steps, as shown in figure 6.

8 Add turquoise beads between the most recent Lazy Daisy Stitches, and sew dark turquoise beads above each inverted teardrop (for beading guidance, see page 32).

Key

● turquoise

● dark turquoise

Two Trees Scrapbook Cover

Add a special touch to any collection of memories.

What You Need

Light green fabric (see step 1 for the amount)

Scrapbook, at least 5 inches square (12.7 cm)

Trees and Squirrel design

Sewing thread to match fabric

Embroidery floss, 1 skein each of brown, green, pale green, yellow green, and light yellow*

*The author used DMC embroidery floss in colors 165, 420, 445, 471, and 3348. The scrapbook shown in the photo is 8 inches square (20.3 cm).

Stitches

Chain Stitch

Straight Stitch

Satin Stitch

Split Stitch

Instructions

1 Measure along the top of the open scrapbook from the outer edge of the front to the outer edge of the back. Add 10 inches (25.4 cm). This is the fabric width for the cover. Measure the scrapbook from the top to the bottom and add 4 inches (10.2 cm). This is the fabric length for the cover. Cut your fabric to these dimensions. There will be extra fabric on all sides: 2 inches (5.1 cm) at both the top and the bottom, and 5 inches (12.7 cm) along each of the sides.

2 Make a ½-inch (1.3 cm) double hem (page 33) at each side.

Trees and Squirrel design

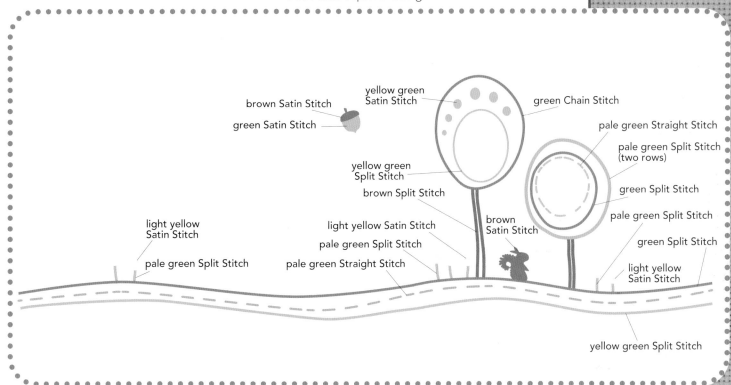

brown Satin Stitch
green Satin Stitch
yellow green Satin Stitch
green Chain Stitch
pale green Straight Stitch
pale green Split Stitch (two rows)
green Split Stitch
pale green Split Stitch
green Split Stitch
light yellow Satin Stitch
yellow green Split Stitch
brown Split Stitch
brown Satin Stitch
light yellow Satin Stitch
light yellow Satin Stitch
pale green Split Stitch
pale green Straight Stitch
pale green Split Stitch
yellow green Split Stitch

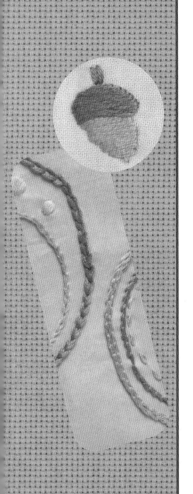

3 Sew a 1½-inch (1.3 cm) hem or ¾-inch (1.9 cm) double hem at the top and bottom edges (figure 1).

4 Enlarge the Trees and Squirrels design to fit the scrapbook cover. Transfer the Trees and Squirrel design to the fabric piece, centering it in the middle of the front. You should have 4 inches (10.2 cm) of extra fabric at both sides. These ends will wrap around the front and back covers. Transfer the acorn to the lower right corner. This image will end up on the inside of the front flap (figure 2).

5 Embroider the design.

6 At each side, fold 4 inches (10.2 cm) to the interior, and pin them in place at the top and bottom edges. Try the cover on the scrapbook. Close the book to ensure the cover fits. If it's too tight or loose, adjust the width of the pocket flaps.

7 Remove the cover from the book. Secure the top and bottom of each flap as folded, along the hemmed edges, by straight-stitching through all layers ⅛ inch (.3 cm) from the edges (figure 2).

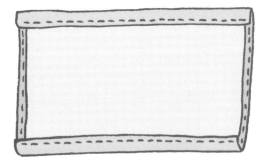

Figure 1

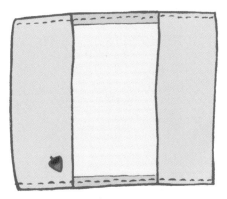

Figure 2

No-Peeking Eye Mask

You'll feel just like a movie star when you pamper yourself with this satin sleep mask.

What You Need

Eyes designs (page 63)

Eye Mask Front, Back, and Back Overlap pattern pieces (page 121)

10-inch square (25.4 cm) of sea green satin fabric

Embroidery floss, 1 skein each of aqua, black, dark plum, light plum, medium plum, and white*

30 inches (76.2 cm) of white ribbon, ½ inch (1.3 cm) wide

9 x 12 inches (22.9 x 30.5 cm) of craft felt

*The author used DMC embroidery floss in colors 310, 598, 3834, 3835, 3836, and white.

Stitches

Long and Short Stitch

Satin Stitch

Split Stitch

Finished Size

7 x 2¾ inches (17.8 x 7 cm), excluding ribbon ties. One size fits most.

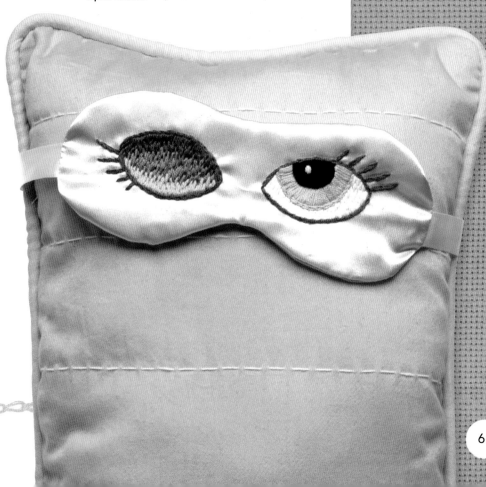

No-Peeking Eye Mask

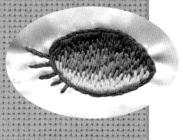

Instructions

1 Trace the Eye Mask pattern pieces on the satin fabric. Don't cut them out yet.

2 Trace the Eyes designs of choice inside the Eye Mask Front that you traced on the fabric. You can embroider two open eyes, two closed eyes, or one of each for a saucy wink.

3 Embroider the design. When working the eyelid, blend the colors while continuing the established rhythm of Long and Short Stitches (page 30). This way, there won't be a solid, straight line between the dark, light, and medium plums.

4 Cut out the Eye Mask Back, Back Overlap, and embroidered Front fabric shapes.

5 Make a ¼-inch (6 mm) double hem (page 33) along the straight ends of each back fabric shape (figure 1).

6 With the right sides facing, position the back pieces over the Front. Place the Back Overlap on top of the Back so that the hemmed edges overlap ½ inch (1.3 cm) (figure 2).

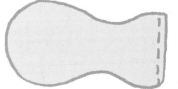

Figure 1

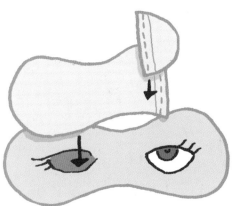

Figure 2

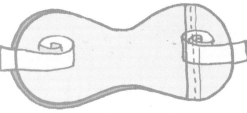

Figure 3

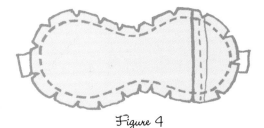

Figure 4

7 Cut the ribbon in half and pin an end of each piece inside the mask. Trap the ribbon between the Front and backs with only one end of each ribbon extending slightly beyond the outer edges of the fabric layers (figure 3). You may need to roll up the ribbon pieces inside, or pull the ends out through the opening where the backs overlap, so that you don't accidentally sew over them. Pin the ribbon edges and fabric shapes together. Sew around the edges of the fabric ½ inch (1.3 cm) from the edges. Don't sew along the hemmed edges.

8 Cut notches in the edges of the fabric, up to—but not through—the stitching line (figure 4). This will help the edges of the mask look smooth when turned. Turn the mask right side out.

9 Trace the Eye Mask Front pattern piece on to the felt and cut it out just inside the tracing line. Slip this inside the mask. This will help keep out that pesky morning light. Rather than felt, you can slide a plastic gel-filled eye mask inside, to give yourself a luxurious treat.

Eyes design

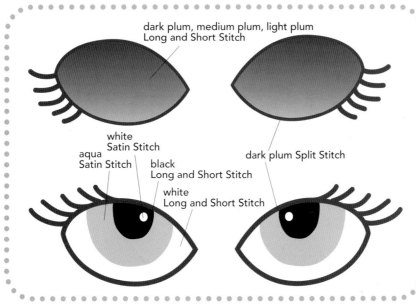

dark plum, medium plum, light plum
Long and Short Stitch

white
Satin Stitch

aqua
Satin Stitch

black
Long and Short Stitch

white
Long and Short Stitch

dark plum Split Stitch

Enlarge 126%

Swirling Scarf

Decorate an airy chiffon scarf with pretty swirls and dots.

What You Need

Chiffon scarf, at least 8 inches (20.3 cm) wide

Nonpermanent fabric marking pen

Swirls and Dots design

Embroidery floss, 1 skein each of coral and light coral*

Self-adhesive, water-soluble fabric stabilizer

The author used DMC embroidery floss in colors 352 and 353.

Stitches

Satin Stitch

Stem Stitch

Instructions

Note: Don't try to embroider chiffon without stabilizer. You'll end up with lots of puckered stitches—or fabric.

1 Place the Swirls and Dots design, face up, on a light table. Place the scarf, also face up, on top, with the outer edges of the design 1 inch (2.5 cm) away from a corner. Secure the layers with strips of the stabilizer, which are sticky but easier to remove than tape. Using the fabric pen, trace the design on the scarf with rows of little dots.

2 Remove the design underneath the scarf. Cut a piece of stabilizer larger than the design and smooth it onto the back of the scarf, keeping the fabric as straight and taut as possible. Don't stretch the fabric. Keep an eye on the swirls in the design to ensure they remain circular.

3 Place the stabilized scarf in the embroidery hoop. If the stabilizer doesn't extend as far as the hoop edges, take extra care hooping the fabric so the fibers aren't damaged. Loosely hoop the fabric by gently pulling the edges, while tightening the screw a little at a time.

4 Embroider the design, starting with the lines that are worked with Stem Stitches. Keep your stitches small and tight, especially around the curves.

5 If desired, repeat the design at the opposite end of the scarf.

6 Soak the scarf in water to remove the stabilizer and design lines. This step also slightly tightens the fabric if it stretched out of shape.

Swirls and Dots design

coral
Stem Stitch

light coral
Satin Stitch

Sea Change Pins

Accessorize clothing, bags, or even curtains with these pretty pins.

What You Need

Stripes designs (page 68)

3 pieces of white cotton fabric, 3½ inches square (8.9 cm)

Embroidery floss, 1 skein each of aqua, light aqua, brown, green, light green, and light sea green*

3½ x 5 inches (8.9 x 12.7 cm) of mat board, heavy card stock, or smooth cardboard

Polyester fiberfill

Glue gun and glue sticks

3 metal pin backs

The author used DMC embroidery floss in colors 420, 471, 472, 598, 747, and 772.

Stitches

Back Stitch

Chain Stitch

French Knot

Straight Stitch

Stem Stitch

Satin Stitch

Split Stitch

Finished Size

1½ inches (3.8 cm) in diameter.

Instructions

1 Transfer all three of the Stripes designs to a piece of fabric, spacing the motifs 2 inches (5.1 cm) apart.

2 Embroider the designs.

3 Cut out each embroidered circle with a ¾-inch (1.9 cm) seam allowance outside the perimeter of every design.

4 From the mat board, cut three large circles with 1½-inch (3.8 cm) diameters and three small circles with 1⅜-inch (3.5 cm) diameters.

5 Turn the stitched fabric circles over so the back side of the embroidery is facing you. Place a small amount of polyester fiberfill (about the size of a grape) in the center of each embroidered fabric circle. Place a large mat board circle on top of each bit of fiberfill (figure 1).

6 Working on one fabric circle at a time, wrap the edges of the fabric around the fiberfill and mat board until the outermost stitching is aligned with the edges of the mat board. Use hot-glue to attach the excess fabric to the mat board circle (figure 2).

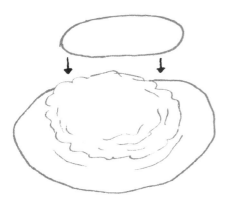

Figure 1

Figure 2

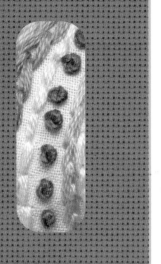

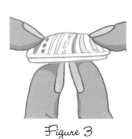

Figure 3

7 Hot glue a smaller circle to the back of each fabric and mat board stack. This will hide the excess fabric. While the glue is still hot, press the layers together, as shown in figure 3, working your fingers around the circle as you press.

8 Glue a pin back to the back of each exposed mat board circle that you applied in step 7.

Stripes design

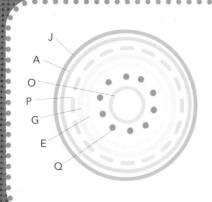

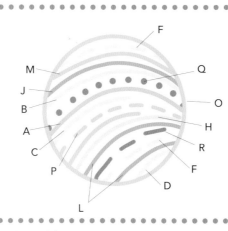

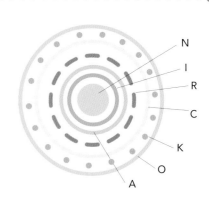

Key

A aqua Split Stitch	J green Chain Stitch
B light aqua Back Stitch	K green French Knot
C light aqua Chain Stitch	L green Split Stitch
D light aqua Split Stitch	M light green Back Stitch
E light aqua Stem Stitch	N light green Satin Stitch
F light aqua Straight Stitch	O light green Split Stitch
G light sea green Back Stitch	P light green Straight Stitch
H light sea green Split Stitch	Q brown French Knot
I green Back Stitch	R brown Straight Stitch

Café Apron

Tie on this fresh little topper the next time you make coffee or tea.

What You Need

⅓ yard (.3 m) of pink cotton fabric

Geometry compass

Nonpermanent fabric marking pen

Sewing thread to match the fabric

Café Cup design (page 71)

Embroidery floss, 1 skein each of cream, dark brown, medium brown, light pink, and pink*

2 yards (1.82 m) of pink satin ribbon, 2 inches (5.1 cm) wide

The author used DMC embroidery floss colors 760, 761, 801, 3862, and ecru.

Stitches

French Knot

Lazy Daisy Stitch

Satin Stitch

Scallop Stitch

Split Stitch

Stem Stitch

Threaded Running Stitch

Finished Size

18 x 12 inches (45.7 x 30.5 cm), excluding ties.

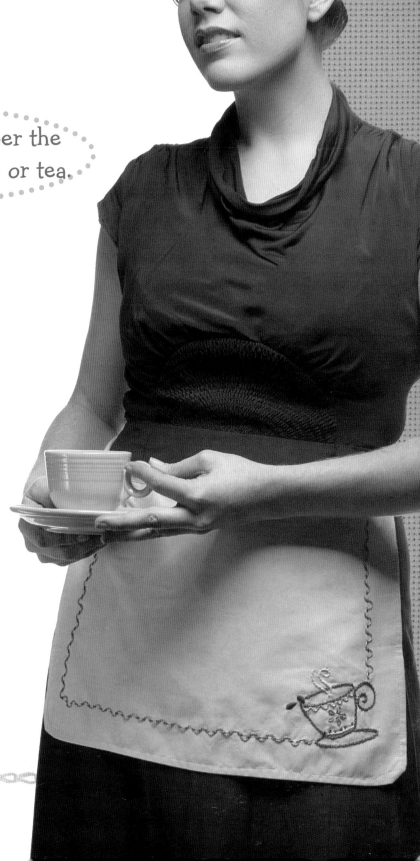

Café Apron...

Instructions

1 Cut two 18 x 12-inch (45.7 x 30.5 cm) rectangles from the fabric. Measure 1½ inches (3.8 cm) from each top corner. Draw a diagonal line from this point to the lower corner on the same side (figure 1). Cut off the sides of the fabric along the lines. Use the geometry compass and fabric pen to round off the two bottom corners. Cut off the corners as marked.

2 Transfer the Café Cup design to the right corner of the wider end of one of the fabric shapes so that the Threaded Running Stitch borders can be stitched 1½ inches (3.8 cm)—or more—in from the side and bottom edges.

3 Embroider the design. Extend the Threaded Running Stitch to the top of the apron on the right hand side, along the bottom, and up the left side (figure 2).

4 Line up the two fabric shapes with the embroidery on the inside and pin them together. Sew around the sides and bottom ½ inch (1.3 cm) in from the edges. Cut small notches in the fabric around the rounded corners, up to—but not through—the stitching line. This will help smooth the edges. Turn the apron right side out and iron the seams flat.

5 Topstitch around the sides and bottom, ½ inch (1.3 cm) in from the edges.

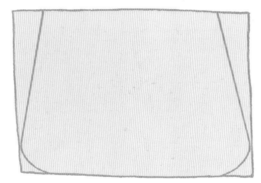

Figure 1

Figure 2

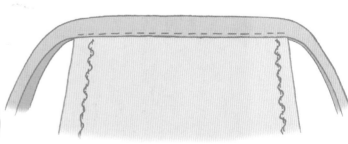

Figure 3

6 Center the ribbon—vertically and horizontally—along the top edge of the apron. You should have an equal amount of ribbon extending beyond both sides, for waist ties. The upper half of the ribbon should extend beyond the upper fabric edge.

7 Fold the ribbon in half lengthwise over the top edge of the fabric, to the underside. Make sure there's an equal amount of ribbon on both sides of the fabric and that the edges are lined up. Pin the ribbon in place and sew it in position through all three of the layers: the front half of the ribbon, the apron fabric, and the back half of the ribbon (figure 3).

Café Cup design

dark brown and pink
Threaded Running Stitch

cream
Split Stitch

dark brown
Split Stitch

dark brown
Satin Stitch

light pink
Scallop Stitch

pink Lazy Daisy Stitch

pink French Knot

medium brown
French Knot

light pink Stem Stitch

dark brown and pink
Threaded Running Stitch

dark brown Split Stitch

Enlarge 134%

Spring Step Shoes

You'll be stepping out in style
wearing embroidered canvas shoes.

What You Need

Bouncing Balls design

White transfer paper

Canvas shoes

Embroidery floss, 1 skein each of
medium pink, pale pink, and cream*

Rubber or leather thimble

*The author used DMC embroidery
floss in colors 776, 818, and ecru.*

Stitches

Satin Stitch

Split Stitch

Instructions

Note: Heavy canvas can be a difficult surface to embroider. It bunches up as you stitch, and it can be so thick that it's difficult to get the needle through. Your fingers will thank you if you use a rubber or leather thimble to help push the needle in and out of the sides of your shoes.

1 Using white transfer paper, transfer the Bouncing Balls design to the side of each shoe. Reverse the image on one shoe, so the motif is positioned the same way on the opposite foot.

2 Embroider the design. If the shoes fit snugly, make your knots as flat as possible so they don't rub against your foot when they're worn. You can end the floss on the outside of the shoe, if desired, by sliding the needle and floss end back and forth underneath the stitching several times before cutting it off. This method for ending floss, however, won't be as secure as a knot made on the back of the work.

Bouncing Balls design

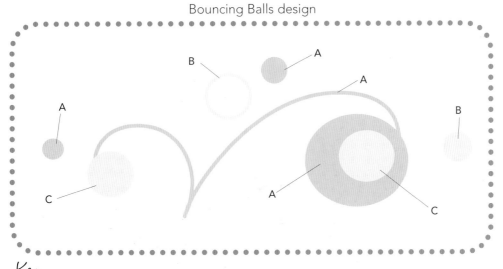

Key
A medium pink
B pale pink
C cream
Use Split Stitch for all lines and Satin Stitch for all circles.

Crazy Curves Headband

Why not make a stylish hand-embroidered headband that's as fun as you are?

What You Need

Curvy Lines design (page 76)

⅛ yard (.11 m) tan cotton fabric

Embroidery floss, 1 skein each of brown, dark brown, coral, light coral, and cream*

5 inches (12.7 cm) of elastic, ½ inch (13 mm) wide

The author used DMC embroidery floss in colors 352, 353, 801, 420, 801, and ecru.

Stitches

Back Stitch

French Knot

Straight Stitch

Satin Stitch

Split Stitch

Long and Short Stitch

Finished Size

2 x 17 inches (5.1 x 43.2 cm), excluding elastic. One size fits most.

Instructions

1 Cut a piece of fabric 4½ x 18 inches (11.4 x 45.7 cm). Find the vertical and horizontal center of the fabric. Transfer two Crazy Curves designs, side by side, in the center of the fabric shape (figure 1).

2 Embroider the designs.

3 Fold the fabric in half lengthwise, with the right side of the embroidery inside. Sew along the matched long edges to make a tube (figure 2). Press the seam allowances open and flat.

4 Turn the tube right side out. Center the seamline in the middle of the tube. With the seamline face up, press the tube flat (figure 3).

5 Fold under ½ inch (1.3 cm) at one end. Position one end of the elastic at the center of this end. Fold in the tube's corners to the inside, over the elastic end (figure 4). Sew a line straight across the fabric and the elastic, going back and forth two or three times to make it secure.

Figure 1

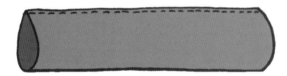

Figure 2

Figure 3

Figure 4

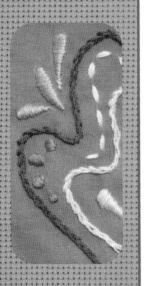

6 Wrap the tube around your head so that the elastic is underneath your hair, at the back of your neck. Pin the loose end of the elastic to the remaining end of the tube so that the headband fits snugly. With the pin still in position, remove the tube from your head. Sew the pinned elastic to the headband.

Key

A dark brown French Knot (3 wraps)
B brown Satin Stitch
C dark brown Split Stitch
D coral Back Stitch
E coral Split Stitch
F coral Satin Stitch
G light coral French Knot
H light coral Split Stitch
I light coral Long and Short Stitch
J light coral Satin Stitch
K cream Split Stitch
L cream Straight Stitch

Curvy Lines design

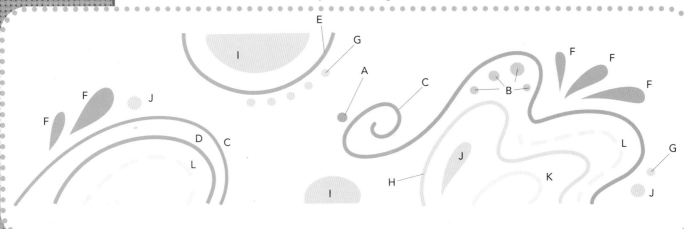

Tag-Along ID Holder

Finding your bag at the airport will be a snap.

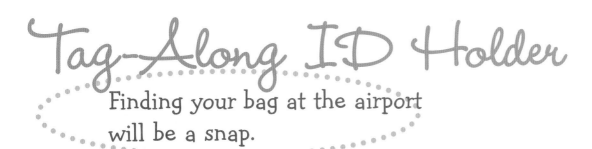

What You Need

Growing design and Casing pattern piece (page 79)

Interior pattern piece (page 122)

9 x 12 inches (22.9 x 30.5 cm) of orange craft felt

Embroidery floss, 1 skein each of coral, light coral, green, and light green*

½-inch (1.3 cm) button

The author used DMC embroidery floss in colors 352, 353, 471, and 472.

Stitches

Feather Stitch

Fly Stitch

French Knot

Satin Stitch

Whip Stitch

Finished Size

3¾ x 2½ inches (9.5 x 6.4 cm), excluding the strap.

Tag-Along I.D. Holder

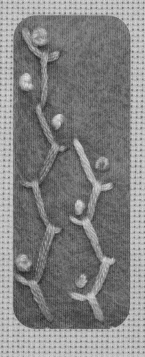

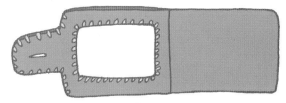

Figure 1

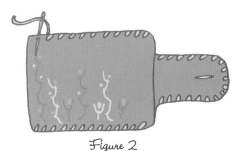

Figure 2

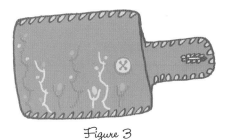

Figure 3

Instructions

Note: You might want to try embroidering without transferring the design to the felt. Just keep in mind that the space nearest the end line will be covered with the strap and button when the finished piece is closed.

1 Transfer the Casing and Interior pattern pieces lines and the design to the felt.

2 Cut each fabric shape from the felt. Cut out the windows as indicated and cut slits for the buttonhole.

3 Embroider the design. You don't need to use a hoop with craft felt.

4 Line up the interior felt piece on the wrong side of the casing and pin it in place. Using the Whip Stitch and a single strand of embroidery floss, join the two shapes around the edge of the strap and the window (figure 1). You can tuck your knots between the two layers of felt to hide them. Leaving the end knotted of the floss with a ½ inch (1.3 cm) long tail will make this easier.

5 Fold the casing along the marked line, with the interior felt shape inside. To join the layers, Whip-stitch along the remaining raw edges (figure 2). Don't stitch the straight, outer edge of the interior shape, which is aligned with the fold line of the casing.

6 Join the layers at the buttonhole by sewing around the edges of the slit with Whip Stitches, keeping the stitches very close together.

7 Sew the button to the embroidered side of the holder, centered ¾ inch (1.9 cm) in from the edge (figure 3).

Growing design and Casing pattern piece

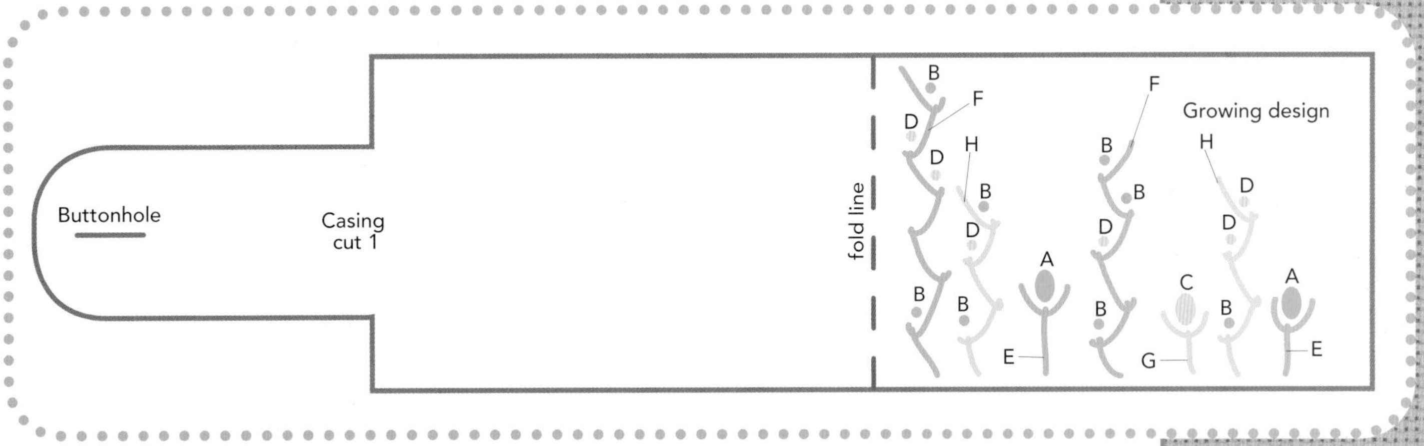

Buttonhole

Casing
cut 1

fold line

Growing design

B
F
D
D
H
B
D
B
B
A
E

F
B
D
B
C
G
H
D
D
A
E

Enlarge 153%

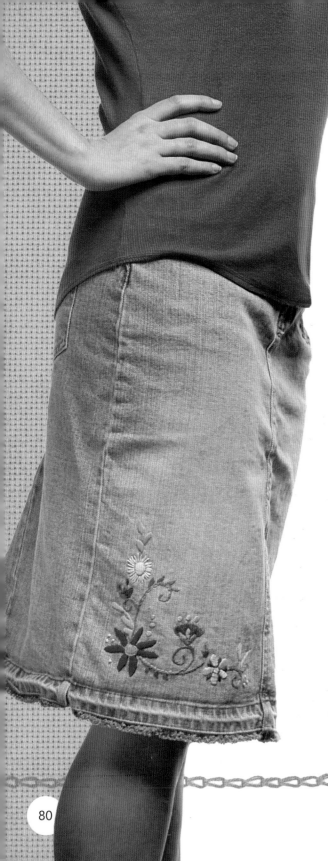

Flower Shop Skirt

Add unique wildflowers to a denim skirt.

What You Need

Wildflowers design

Plain denim skirt

White transfer paper

Nonpermanent fabric marking pen

Embroidery floss, 1 skein each of aqua, pale blue, bright green, lime green, teal green, coral, dark coral, light coral, medium orange, purple, red, and yellow*

The author used DMC embroidery floss in colors 321, 327, 351, 352, 353, 598, 701, 727, 907, 3753, 3849, and 3854.

Stitches

Back Stitch

French Knot

Satin Stitch

Split Stitch

Straight Stitch

Instructions

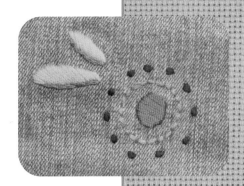

Note: Keep your stitches tight and close together to help prevent them from snagging when your skirt is washed.

1 Using white transfer paper, transfer the main part of the Wildflowers design to the lower corner of the skirt. Transfer the extra flower to a front or back pocket. Go over the lines with the fabric pen.

2 Embroider the design, moving the hoop around on the denim as needed until you've stitched it all. Lightly press out any wrinkles from the inside of the skirt.

Wildflowers design

Enlarge 119%

Key

A lime green Satin Stitch
B lime green Back Stitch
C bright green Satin Stitch
D bright green Split Stitch
E bright green Back Stitch
F pale blue Straight Stitch
G pale blue French Knot (3 wraps)
H teal green Satin Stitch
I aqua Satin Stitch
J coral Satin Stitch
K coral Back Stitch
L medium orange Satin Stitch
M medium orange Split Stitch
N red Satin Stitch
O purple Satin Stitch
P purple Straight Stitch
Q dark coral Satin Stitch
R light coral Satin Stitch
S yellow Satin Stitch

"Wooden" Pincushion

Lift your spirits by embroidering, and then hand-sewing, this easy faux wood grain design.

What You Need

Wood Grain Top design and pattern piece (page 84)

Wood Grain Side design (page 84)

9 x 12 inches (22.9 x 30.5 cm) of tan craft felt

White or blue transfer paper

Embroidery floss, 1 skein each of brown and dark brown*

Polyester fiberfill

The author used DMC embroidery floss in colors 420 and 801.

Stitches

Split Stitch

Whip Stitch

Finished Size

1½ inches (3.8 cm) deep, 2½ inches (6.4 cm) in diameter, 7 inches (17.8 cm) in circumference.

Instructions

Note: You can make your own matching nature pins with a bit of polymer clay, some straight pins with metal heads, and acrylic craft paint.

1 Transfer the Wood Grain designs and pincushion patterns to the felt.

2 Embroider the designs. You don't need to use a hoop with craft felt. Following the pattern lines, cut out each shape from the felt. Also cut a 2½-inch (6.4 cm) diameter felt circle for the bottom.

3 Butt together the short ends of the Side fabric shape. Whip-stitch the ends together with one ply of brown embroidery floss (figure 1).

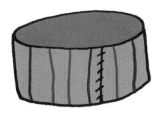

Figure 1

4 Sew the bottom fabric shape to the lower edge of the side piece, again using Whip Stitches and a ply of brown embroidery floss (figure 2).

5 Stuff polyester fiberfill into the partially assembled pincushion until you have a mound above the side.

Figure 2

6 Sew on the embroidered top, using Whip Stitches and a ply of brown embroidery floss. Gently push on the fiberfill as you stitch (figure 3).

Figure 3

Wood Grain Top design

Enlarge 110%

Key
A brown Split Stitch
B dark brown Split Stitch

Wood Grain Top design

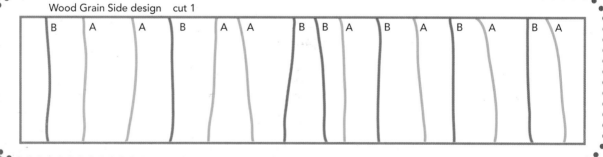

Wood Grain Side design   cut 1

B A   A   B   A   A   B B A   B   A   B   A   B A

Enlarge 110%

Night Sky Bookmarks

Stitching directly on paper gives these bookmarks a unique look.

What You Need

4 x 6½ inches (10.2 x 16.5 cm) of watercolor paper or heavy card stock with a textured surface

Lead pencil

Goodnight Moon design (page 86)

Hanging Stars design (page 87)

Embroidery floss, 1 skein each of aqua, light aqua, dark periwinkle, periwinkle, and light blue*

Hole punch

*The author used DMC embroidery floss in colors 340, 341, 747, and 3753. The author used 140-lb. (300 g) white, cold-press watercolor paper.

Stitches

Cross Stitch Star Stitch

French Knot

Satin Stitch

Split Stitch

Straight Stitch

Finished Size

2 x 6½ inches (5.1 x 16.5 cm).

Night Sky Bookmarks

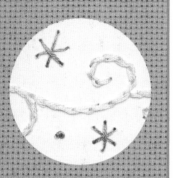

Instructions

1 Transfer the Goodnight Moon and Hanging Stars designs to a piece of paper, just as you would place a design on fabric. (Don't, however, use the Transfer Pencil Method.) If the decorative paper has an interesting raw edge, you might want to position the designs to take advantage of this.

2 Embroider the design. Stitching on paper is different from working on fabric, but it's easy to get the hang of it. Most heavy paper is fairly forgiving. Start and end each length of floss with a knot. You might find it difficult to determine where your needle will poke through the paper from the back. You may need to keep your stitches slightly farther apart, to prevent the floss from ripping the paper between the holes. Here's an easy trick: Come up from the underside, pushing gently on the needle until you see a tiny bump start to rise on the front of the paper; if the needle is in the wrong place, you can move it without leaving a visible puncture in the paper. If you accidentally poke a hole in the wrong place, smooth it with your fingernail or the tip of

Goodnight Moon design

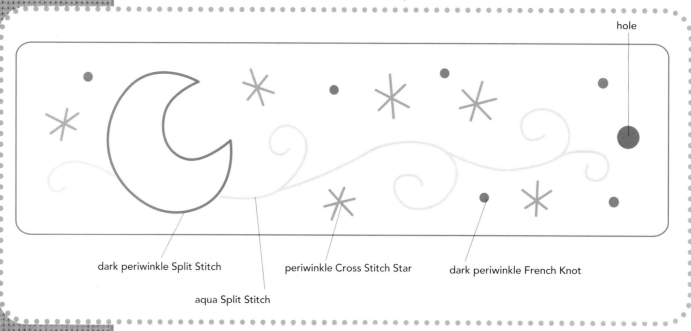

hole

dark periwinkle Split Stitch

aqua Split Stitch

periwinkle Cross Stitch Star

dark periwinkle French Knot

the needle. Keep your index fingers close to the needle as you pass it through the paper to prevent it from bending.

3 Punch a hole in the paper in the spot indicated on each design. For each bookmark tassel, loop a 9-inch (22.9 cm) length of floss through the hole (figure 1). Knot the ends and separate the plies.

Figure 1

Hanging Stars design

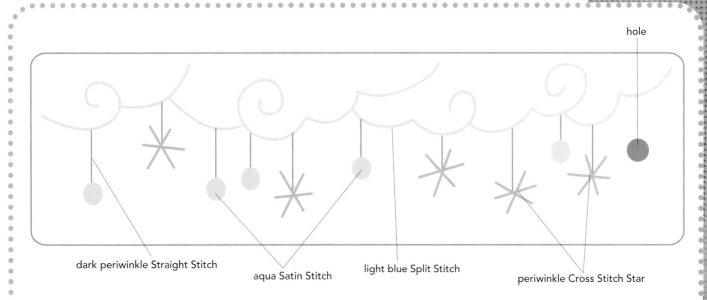

hole

dark periwinkle Straight Stitch

aqua Satin Stitch

light blue Split Stitch

periwinkle Cross Stitch Star

Boxer Shorts

What's more fitting to stitch on boxer shorts?

Boxer design

light brown Long and Short Stitch

brown Satin Stitch

black Satin Stitch

dark brown Split Stitch

black Satin Stitch

cream Long and Short Stitch

black Straight Stitch

brown Split Stitch

medium pink Satin Stitch

cream Long and Short Stitch

cream Split Stitch

light brown Long and Short Stitch

What You Need

Cotton boxer shorts

Boxer design

Embroidery floss, 1 skein each of black, brown, dark brown, light brown, cream, and medium pink*

*The author used DMC embroidery floss in colors 310, 420, 422, 776, 801, and ecru.

Stitches

Long and Short Stitch

Satin Stitch

Split Stitch

Straight Stitch

Instructions

1. Transfer the Boxer pattern to the front of the boxer shorts.

2. Embroider the design, starting with the outlines in Split Stitch, and then filling in the solid areas with Long and Short Stitches and Satin Stitches.

Zen Lampshade

Bring wishes for good luck, happiness, and creativity into your home with Asian-inspired embroidery.

What You Need

Asian Motifs design

Cloth lampshade without a plastic lining

Carbon paper or thin-lead pencil for tracing the pattern

Embroidery floss, 1 skein each of black, coral red, medium orange, coral, pink, light pink, dark plum, medium plum, pale green, and white*

The author used DMC embroidery floss in colors 310, 351, 352, 722, 761, 3348, 3712, 3834, 3835, 3836, 3854, and white.

Stitches

French Knot

Lazy Daisy Stitch

Satin Stitch

Scallop Stitch

Split Stitch

Straight Stitch

Instructions

1 Copy the Asian Motifs design.

2 Transfer the design using carbon paper so that you can brush off the marks when you've finished embroidering. You could trace the design onto the lampshade with a regular lead pencil since the thin lines will be completely covered by your embroidery stitches. For some variety

in the design, you can cut the images apart and place them in different positions around the lampshade.

3 Your lampshade is already stretched on a frame, so you don't need a hoop. Just start embroidering the design. The design has thick and thin lines. Stitch with 6 plies of floss when working thick lines, and 3 plies for thin lines.

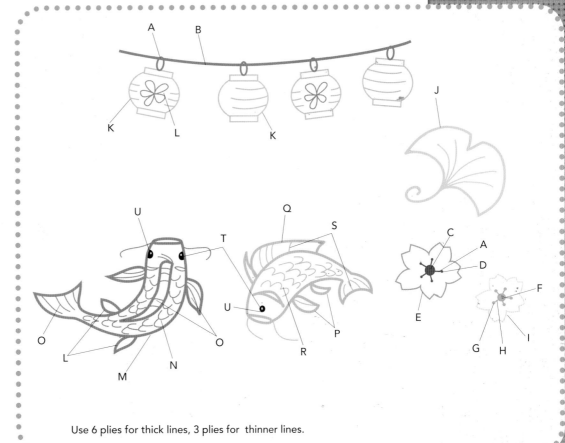

Asian Motifs design

Key

A dark plum Straight Stitch
B dark plum Split Stitch
C dark plum Satin Stitch
D dark plum French Knot
E medium plum Split Stitch
F pink Satin Stitch
G pink French Knot
H pink Straight Stitch
I light pink Split Stitch
J pale green Split Stitch
K coral Split Stitch
L coral red Lazy Daisy
M coral red Split Stitch
N coral red Scallop Stitch
O coral red Straight Stitch
P medium orange Lazy Daisy
Q medium orange Split Stitch
R medium orange Scallop Stitch
S medium orange Straight Stitch
T black Satin Stitch
U white French Knot

Use 6 plies for thick lines, 3 plies for thinner lines.

Nightingale Lap Quilt

A quilt is the perfect surface to embroider, and it doesn't have to be difficult to make. Just use a simple piecing method and some appliqués.

What You Need

1⅜ yards (1.2 m) white cotton fabric

Solid or patterned cotton fabrics, ½ yard (.46 m) light pink, dark pink, and white; ⅝ yard (.57 m) medium pink; ¼ yard (.23 m) red; and ⅓ yard (.3 m) ecru

Rotary cutter, see-through acrylic ruler, and self-healing cutting mat (optional)

Sewing thread to match fabrics

Birds designs (page 101)

Birds and Flowers design (page 97)

Embroidery floss, 2 skeins each of berry red, light pink, and pink; 1 skein each of coral, dark coral, and dark pink*

36 x 46 inches (91.4 x 116.8 cm) of quilt batting

Safety pins

4 yards (3.64 m) of red quilt binding, 1 inch (2.5 cm) finished width

The author used DMC embroidery floss in colors 304, 351, 352, 760, 761, and 3712.

Stitches

French Knot

Chain Stitch

Long and Short Stitch

Scallop Stitch

Split Stitch

Straight Stitch

Finished Size

40 x 30 inches
(101.6 x 76.2 cm).

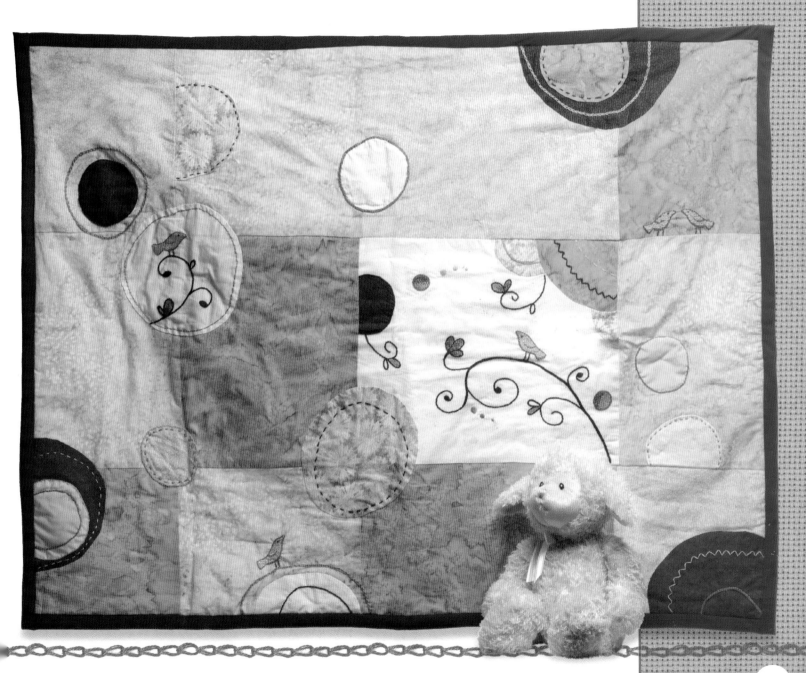

Fabric Appliqués and Blocks Cutting Table

Fabric Color*	Blocks**		Circles Appliqués	
	Amount	Dimensions	Amount	Dimensions
Light pink	1	9 x 11 inches (22.9 x 27.9 cm)	2	5 inches (12.7 cm)
	1	15 x 11 inches (38.1 x 27.9 cm)	1	7 inches (17.8 cm)
	1	9 inches square (22.9 cm)		
Medium pink	1	11 inches square (27.9 cm)	1	8 inches (20.3 cm)
	2	9 x 13 inches (22.9 x 33 cm)	1	7 inches (17.8 cm)
	1	11 x 9 inches (27.9 x 22.9 cm)		
Dark pink	1	9 x 11 inches (22.9 x 27.9 cm)	1	8 inches (20.3 cm)
	1	11 x 13 inches (27.9 x 33 cm)	1	7 inches (17.8 cm)
	1	9 inches square (22.9 cm)		
	1	15 x 9 inches (38.1 x 22.9 cm)		
Red			1	9 inches (22.9 cm)
			2	7 inches (17.8 cm)
			2	5 inches (12.7 cm)
Ecru			1	6 inches (15.2 cm)
			1	10 inches (25.4 cm)
			2	5 inches (12.7 cm)
White	1	15 x 13 inches (38.1 x 33 cm)	1	9 inches (22.9 cm)
			2	7 inches (17.8 cm)
			1	5 inches (12.7 cm)

*If desired, mix and match the prints and solids in each color category.

**The measurements already include a ½-inch (1.3 cm) seam allowance on each side.

Block Assembly Instructions

1 Cut out the quilt blocks according to the Fabric Appliqués and Blocks Cutting Table (at left) and the Block Assembly Guide (figure 1). Keep the rectangle edges as straight as possible. If you have a rotary cutter and cutting mat, they'll come in handy for this job. If you like perfectly uniform circles, you can use a geometry compass to measure them. If you like things a little more organic, just cut them out freehand.

Block Assembly Guide

Figure 1

2 Lay out your blocks on a large, flat surface. Cut out the circle appliqués listed in the Fabric Appliqués and Blocks Cutting Table (page 94). Trim some of the fabric circles to make ovals and cut off the tops of others, as shown in figure 2. Position the circles on top of the blocks.

3 Sew together the background blocks, starting with the top row, and using ½-inch (1.3 cm) seam allowances throughout

the piecing. In some cases, you'll add fabric circles while sewing together adjacent blocks. Refer to figure 2 to identify these circles. They're the the ones that look like an edge has been cut off along a seamline: the light peach circle on the second block from the upper left, for example. (Circles that are appliquéd after the block assembly cover the seamlines.) To create this effect, simply insert the circle between the block as follows: Line up the edges of two adjacent blocks, with

Figure 2

right sides facing and the circle sandwiched inside (figure 3). Now make the seam through all three fabric layers.

4 Continue adding blocks until you finish the first row. Separately sew together each row of blocks in the same way. Press all of the seam allowances in the same direction.

5 Line up the bottom edge of the first row and the upper edge of the second row, with the right sides facing, and sew them together (figure 4). Sew the top of the third, bottom row to the bottom of the second row, in the same way. Press the seam allowances toward the bottom of the quilt. You've completed the patchwork part of your quilt top.

Figure 3

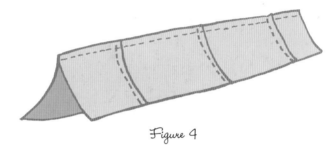

Figure 4

Birds and Flowers design

Key
A   light pink Long and Short Stitch
B   light pink Satin Stitch
C   pink Long and Short Stitch
D   pink Satin Stitch
E   dark pink Split Stitch
F   coral Long and Short Stitch
G   dark coral Long and Short Stitch
H   dark coral Split Stitch
I   berry red Satin Stitch
J   berry red Split Stitch
K   berry red French Knot

Enlarge 350%

Embroidery and Appliqué Instructions

1 Transfer the Birds and Flowers design (page 97) to the white block and the individual Birds designs to the surrounding quilt areas. Appliqué the pieces to the patchwork (figure 5).

2 Embroider the designs.

berry red Straight Stitch

pink Chain Stitch

light pink Split Stitch

pink Split Stitch

berry red Straight Stitch

pink Chain Stitch

pink Split Stitch

light pink Straight Stitch

berry red Scallop Stitch

pink Split Stitch

light pink Straight Stitch

light pink Scallop Stitch

pink Straight Stitch

berry red Split Stitch

berry red Straight Stitch

pink Split Stitch

pink Split Stitch

pink Chain Stitch

light pink Straight Stitch

Quilting Instructions

1 Now you'll make the "quilt sandwich." Measure and cut a piece of batting and a piece of white fabric for the backing. You want the batting and fabric to extend 2 to 3 inches (5.1 to 7.6 cm) beyond all edges of the quilt top. You can join several pieces of white fabric to make the back, or use one large piece of material.

2 On a large, flat surface such as a table or the floor, spread out your quilt backing, face down. You may find it helpful to tape the edges of the backing to the flat surface, to keep it smooth. Spread out the batting on top of the backing, and the quilt top, face up, on top. Find the center of the quilt. Insert a safety pin through all three of the layers to hold them together. Moving out from the center, continue smoothing the layers flat and putting a pin through the layers every 4 to 6 inches (10.2 to 15.2 cm). Once you've finished pinning the quilt pieces together, you can move the work around or hold it in your lap as you finish the quilting.

3 The easiest way to "quilt" a quilt is to tie the layers together with short lengths of embroidery floss. Starting at one end of the quilt, pass the threaded needle through the layers, from top to bottom and then bottom to top, to make a small stitch.

Tie the floss in a tight double knot and trim the ends to ½ inch (1.3 cm), as shown in figure 6. Or you can choose to make the knots on the back of the quilt instead. If you choose to keep the knots on the back, use floss that matches the color squares on the front, so your ties will be barely noticeable.

4 Continue making ties all over the quilt, every 4 inches (10.2 cm). Scatter the ties in a random pattern, or keep them in rows if you prefer. When you've finished tying your quilt, remove all the safety pins.

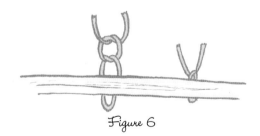

Figure 6

Binding Instructions

1 Cut two pieces of binding, each the same length as the long side of the quilt top, and two pieces 3 inches (7.6 cm) longer than the short side.

2 Unfold (don't press) a piece of binding for a long side and line up one raw edge of the binding with a long edge of the quilt top, with the right sides facing each another. Pin the binding in place and sew along the fold nearest the edge (figure 7).

3 Trim off the extra batting and backing so that the quilt edge is even with the edge of the binding. Fold the loose lengthwise edge of the binding over the edge of the quilt and attach it to the backing using the Appliqué Stitch (figure 8).

4 Attach the remaining long piece of binding to the other long side of the quilt.

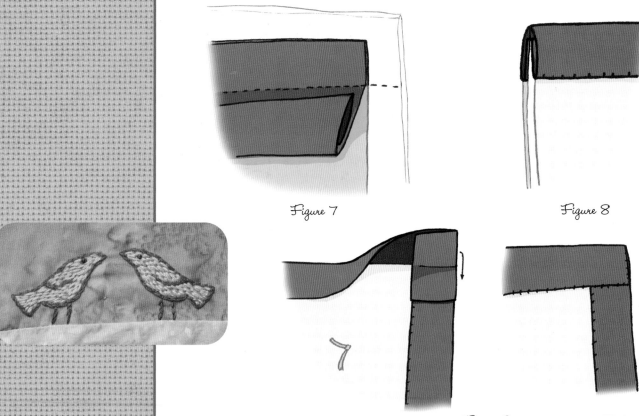

Figure 7

Figure 8

Figure 9

5 Line up a short piece of the binding with a short side of the quilt, letting the ends of the binding hang over each end by 1½ inches (3.8 cm). Sew on the first lengthwise edge the same way you did the long sides.

6 Before you begin stitching the remaining long edge of the binding to the back of the quilt, unfold a short end and tuck in the raw end, to the back of the quilt, so that it wraps over the corner. Fold the long edge of the binding back in place and stitch the end closed. Continue stitching down the long edge (figure 9). Stop stitching 2 inches (5.1 cm) from the end so that you can wrap the end of the binding around the next corner in the same way. Finish the remaining edge in the same way. Congratulations, you've finished your quilt!

Birds designs

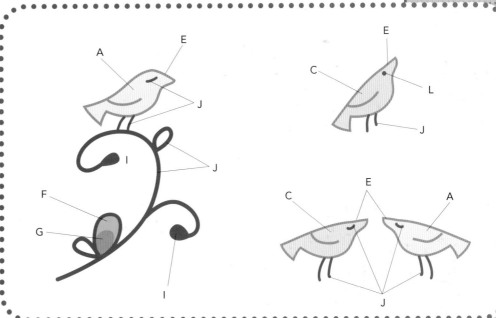

Key

A   light pink Long and Short Stitch
B   light pink Satin Stitch
C   pink Long and Short Stitch
D   pink Satin Stitch
E   dark pink Split Stitch
F   coral Long and Short Stitch
G   dark coral Long and Short Stitch
H   dark coral Split Stitch
I   berry red Satin Stitch
J   berry red Split Stitch
K   berry red French Knot

Sweet Dreams Baby Pillow

Legend has it that you can see
a bunny in the face of every full moon.
What a wonderful bedtime story!

What You Need

10-inch square (25.4 cm) of medium-weight or heavyweight cream cotton fabric

Bunny Moon design

Embroidery floss, 1 skein each of aqua, dark aqua, light aqua, beige, light beige, and cream*

10-inch square (25.4 cm) of aqua patterned flannel fabric

Polyester fiberfill

The author used DMC embroidery floss in colors 597, 598, 747, 822, 3032, and ecru.

Stitches

Chain Stitch

Straight Stitch

Satin Stitch

Split Stitch

Finished Size

10 inches square (25.4 cm).

Instructions

1 Transfer the Bunny Moon design to the center of the cream fabric.

2 Embroider the design.

3 With the right sides facing, pin together the flannel square and the embroidered piece. Sew around the edges, using a 1-inch (2.5 cm) seam allowance and leaving a 2-inch (5.1 cm) opening between the beginning and end of the stitching line. Diagonally clip off the excess seam allowances at the corners, so that the corners look smoother when turned.

4 Turn the pillow right side out through the opening. Stuff polyester fiberfill into the pillow through the opening.

5 Stitch the opening closed using the Hidden Stitch.

Bunny Moon design

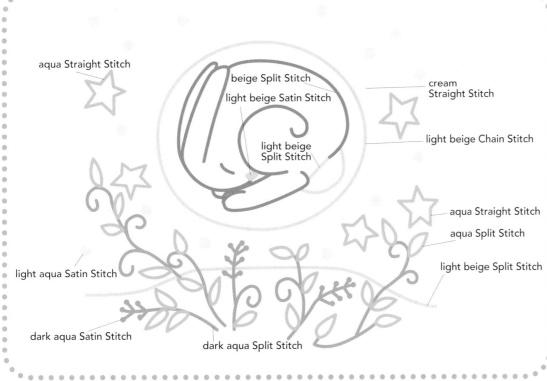

aqua Straight Stitch

beige Split Stitch

light beige Satin Stitch

cream Straight Stitch

light beige Chain Stitch

light beige Split Stitch

aqua Straight Stitch

aqua Split Stitch

light beige Split Stitch

light aqua Satin Stitch

dark aqua Satin Stitch

dark aqua Split Stitch

Enlarge 143%

White-on-White Storage Bag

Your scarves and sweaters will sleep in style.

What You Need

19½ x 25½ inches (49.5 x 64.8 cm) of 100-percent cotton organza

Sewing thread to match fabric

Round Flowers design

Thin-lead pencil

Seam gauge

Tracing paper, 5 inches square (12.7 cm)

Rayon embroidery floss, 1 skein of white*

Liquid seam sealer

The author used DMC rayon embroidery floss in color 35200.

Stitches

Back Stitch

Chain Stitch

Straight Stitch

Satin Stitch

Split Stitch

Finished Size

11⅞ x 17⅝ inches (30.1 x 44.76 cm).

Instructions

Note: If your organza has cotton content, it can be ironed on the iron's cotton setting without using a protective cloth. If your organza has a different fiber content, be sure to test the temperature of your iron on a fabric scrap to avoid scorching the material for your project.

1 Mark a parallel line 5¾ inches (14.6 cm) away from one of the longer sides. Fold the fabric along that line. Press along the fold, pin it, and then Straight-stitch parallel to the fold, through both layers, ¼ inch (6 mm) from the fold. Press the seamline flat, with the fold to one side.

2 Fold the fabric right side out, matching the edges of the short sides. Straight-stitch ³⁄₁₆ inch (5 mm) away from the edge to create a tube. Turn the tube wrong side out and press it with the seamline at the edge. To make a French seam, stitch ¼ inch (6 mm) away from the previous seamline, trapping the previous seam allowance inside the new seam allowance. Press the finished seam with the enclosed seam allowance to one side.

Round Flowers design

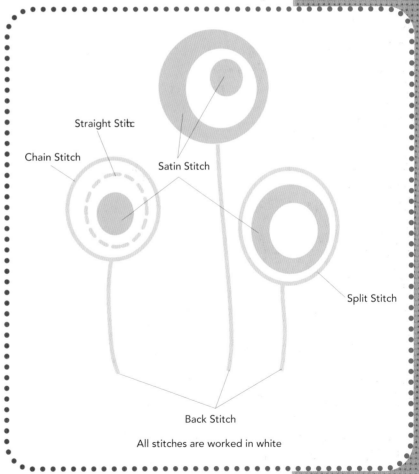

Straight Stitc

Chain Stitch

Satin Stitch

Split Stitch

Back Stitch

All stitches are worked in white

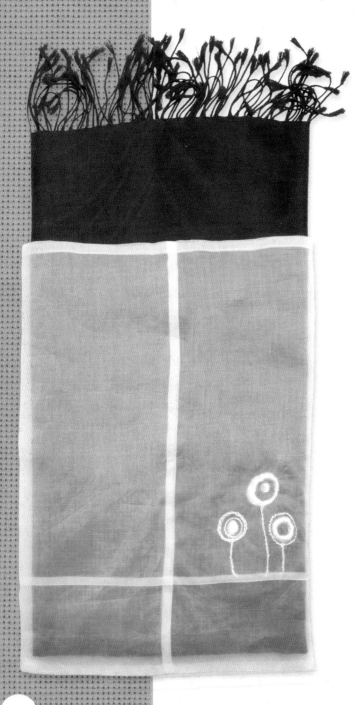

3 Arrange the tube, right side out, so the vertical seam is centered, rather than to one side. The bottom (closed) edge will be the one nearest the horizontal seam that you made in step 1. Pin the bottom, matching the edges, and stitch ³⁄₁₆ inch (5 mm) from the edges. Turn the piece wrong side out and press it. Finish the French seam by stitching ¼ inch (6 mm) away from the previous seam. Press the finished seam with the enclosed seam allowance to one side.

4 Make a ¼-inch (6 mm) double hem (page 33) at the top of the bag.

5 Turn the bag right side out. Copy the Round Flowers design (page 105) to the tracing paper. You won't need any special tools to transfer it onto the bag, because organza is thin enough to see through. Just place the pattern behind the bag on the right side above the seam and trace it with a pencil.

6 Embroider the design. Rayon floss has a smooth, satin-like surface, but it can be slick and cause knots to slip loose. To keep your knots tight, put a small dab of liquid seam sealer on each one.

Perfect Paisley Pillowcase

This is an easy design to adapt to different projects. You can use all the motifs in a row or scatter them at random.

What You Need

Paisley design (page 109)

Lavender cotton pillowcase

Embroidery floss, 1 skein each of coral, light coral, dark plum, light plum, and medium plum*

The author used DMC embroidery floss in colors 352, 353, 3834, 3835, and 3836.

Stitches

Center Point Star Stitch

French Knot

Lazy Daisy Stitch

Satin Stitch

Scallop Stitch

Split Stitch

Straight Stitch

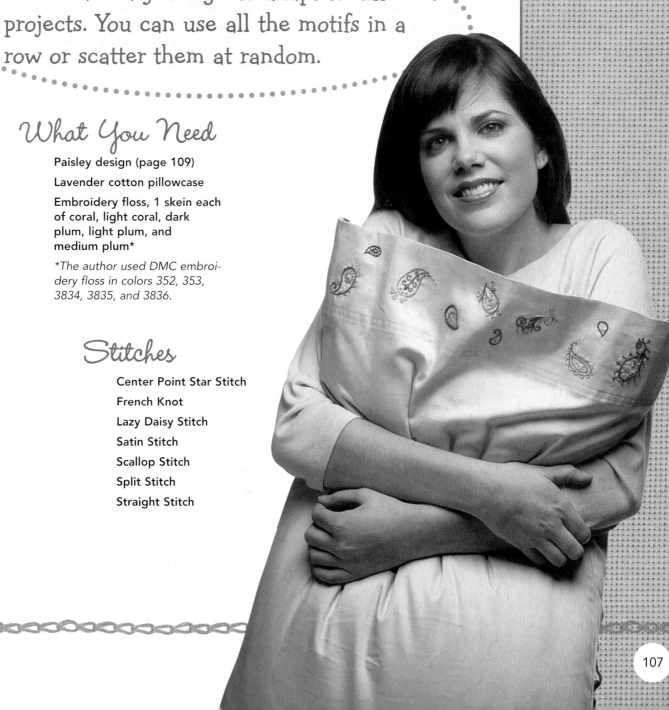

Instructions

1 Copy the Paisley design onto the transfer paper, at the same time creating one continuous design by overlapping the right edge of the upper portion of the design on the left edge of bottom portion.

2 Embroider the design. The thick lines on the design are embroidered using all six plies of floss. Use three of the six plies for the thinner lines.

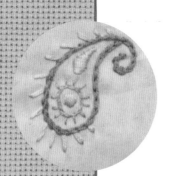

Key

A coral French Knot
B coral Center Point Star
C coral Satin Stitch
D coral Split Stitch
E coral Straight Stitch
F light coral French Knot
G light coral Satin Stitch
H light coral Straight Stitch
I dark plum French Knot
J dark plum Satin Stitch
K dark plum Split Stitch
L dark plum Straight Stitch
M light plum Scallop Stitch
N light plum Lazy Daisy Stitch
O light plum Satin Stitch
P light plum Split Stitch
Q medium plum French Knot
R medium plum Satin Stitch
S medium plum Split Stitch
T medium plum Straight Stitch

Paisley design

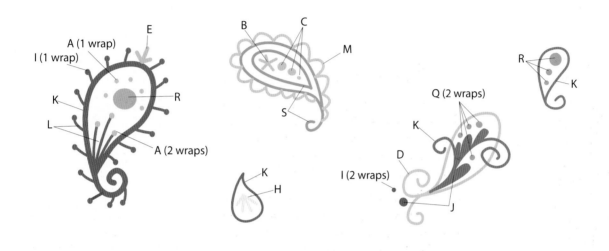

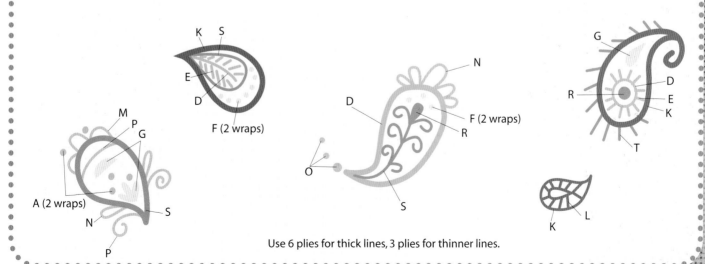

Use 6 plies for thick lines, 3 plies for thinner lines.

Mod Napkins

The dinner table will be fashionably outfitted with these retro embroidered napkins.

What You Need

Circles and Dots design

20-inch square (50.8 cm) linen napkins

Embroidery floss, 1 skein each of aqua and red*

The author used DMC embroidery floss in colors 321 and 598.

Stitches

Satin Stitch

Split Stitch

Instructions

Note: You can make a different version of this pattern by flipping it around and switching which shapes are red and aqua.

1 Transfer the Circles and Dots design to a corner of each napkin.

2 Embroider the design.

Key
A aqua
B red

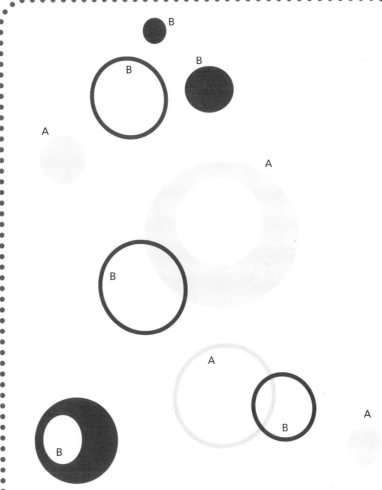

Note: All lines are Split Stitch and all solid colors are Satin Stitch

Enlarge 135%

Flowering Vines...Ribbons

You'll find all kinds of uses for these pretty embroidered ribbons.

What You Need

Vines and Flowers designs

Lengths of blue and green grosgrain ribbon, 1 inch (2.5 cm) wide

Embroidery floss, 1 skein each of light plum, medium plum, lime green, and white*

The author used DMC embroidery floss in colors 907, 3835, 3836, and white.

Stitches

French Knot

Lazy Daisy Stitch

Split Stitch

Instructions

1 Cut a piece of ribbon the length you need and then transfer the Vines and Flowers design onto one side (the front) of each ribbon. You'll have to repeat the design over and over along the ribbon's length.

2 Stretch the ribbon across the middle of your embroidery hoop and embroider the design.

Vines and Flowers design

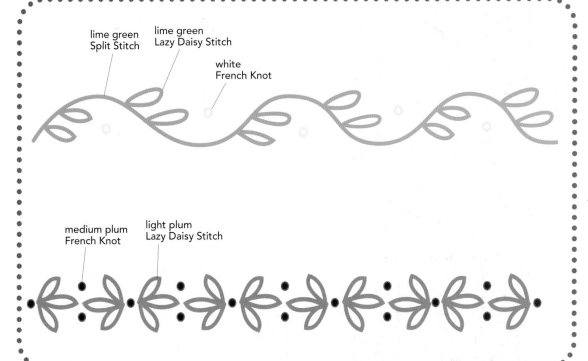

lime green
Split Stitch

lime green
Lazy Daisy Stitch

white
French Knot

medium plum
French Knot

light plum
Lazy Daisy Stitch

Fireworks Halter Top

Starbursts of French Knots and Satin Stitches look like colorful fireworks in the night sky.

What You Need

Starbursts design

Black cotton halter top

White transfer paper

Fabric stabilizer

Embroidery floss, 1 skein each of dark coral, medium orange, and red*

*The author used DMC embroidery floss in colors 321, 351, and 3854.

Stitches

French Knot

Satin Stitch

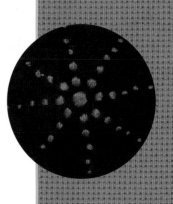

Instructions

1 Using white transfer paper, transfer the Starbursts design to the halter. Try on the halter top after you transfer the design and before you begin embroidering, to make sure that none of the stitching will end up accentuating a part of your figure that you don't want people to notice.

2 Cut a piece of fabric stabilizer larger than the pattern and apply it to the inside of the halter at the design area.

3 Embroider the design. You've done a bang-up job!

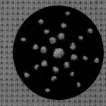

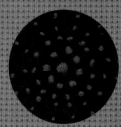

Starbursts design

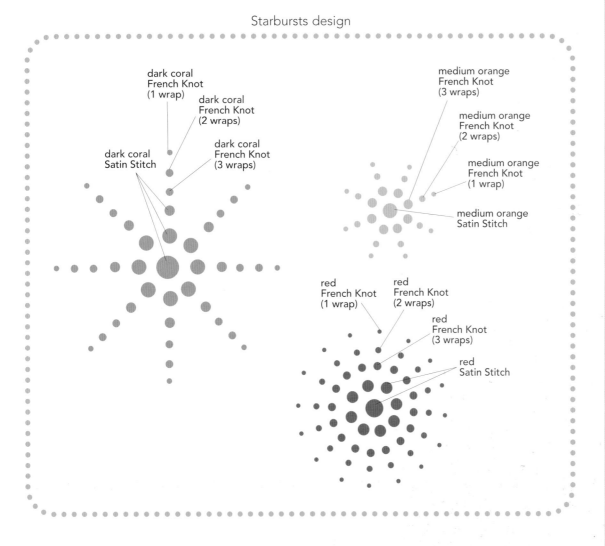

dark coral
French Knot
(1 wrap)

dark coral
French Knot
(2 wraps)

dark coral
Satin Stitch

dark coral
French Knot
(3 wraps)

medium orange
French Knot
(3 wraps)

medium orange
French Knot
(2 wraps)

medium orange
French Knot
(1 wrap)

medium orange
Satin Stitch

red
French Knot
(1 wrap)

red
French Knot
(2 wraps)

red
French Knot
(3 wraps)

red
Satin Stitch

Lucky Number Jeans

Put on these jeans to have a lucky day!

What You Need

Blue jeans

Embroidery floss, 1 skein each of dark periwinkle, periwinkle, and light blue violet*

White carbon paper

Nonpermanent fabric marking pen

Numbers design

The author used DMC embroidery floss in colors 340, 341, and 3747.

Stitches

Chain Stitch

Satin Stitch

Split Stitch

Finished Size

To fit a pocket more than 4 inches square (10.2 cm).

Instructions

1 Transfer your favorite number design to a back pocket using white carbon paper. Trace the pattern with the fabric pen.

2 Embroider the design. You probably won't need to use an embroidery hoop. As you work, periodically open the pocket, to make sure that you aren't stitching it shut.

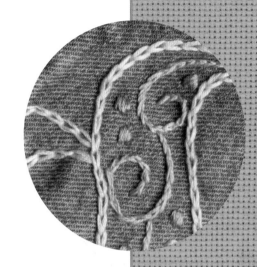

Numbers design

light blue violet
Chain Stitch

dark periwinkle
Satin Stitch

periwinkle
Split Stitch

Enlarge 280%

Mine All Mine Towel

Give your towel a
dazzling personality.

What You Need

Mine design (page 120)

Bath towel with a smooth surface (low nap), at least 20 inches (50.8 cm) wide

White carbon paper

Nonpermanent white fabric marking pen

Embroidery floss, 2 skeins of light purple and 1 skein of metallic silver*

The author used DMC embroidery floss in colors 3743 and Light Effects (Jewel) E168.

Stitches

Center Point Star Stitch

Satin Stitch

Straight Stitch

Instructions

Note: Metallic thread will make your design extra sparkly. It can be difficult to work with, however, so it's better to use it only for accents, such as the stars in this design.

1 Using white carbon paper, transfer the Mine design to one end of the towel, centering it in the border area 1 to 2 inches (2.5 to 5.1 cm) from the edge. You may find transferring the design onto a fluffy towel challenging. Be sure to work on a hard surface and don't worry if your carbon paper tears. After you get the basic shapes onto the towel, trace over the transferred marks with the fabric pen.

2 Embroider the design. Notice how the direction of the lines of Satin Stitches change as the lines curve and become thicker and thinner. You want your stitching to do the same as you work along the lines. You may want to stitch over the lines twice to make them stand out against the long fibers of the terry cloth.

Mine design

light purple Satin Stitch

stars for left side

metallic silver Straight Stitch

metallic silver Center Point Star Stitch

stars for right side

Patterns

No-Peeking Eye Mask (page 61)

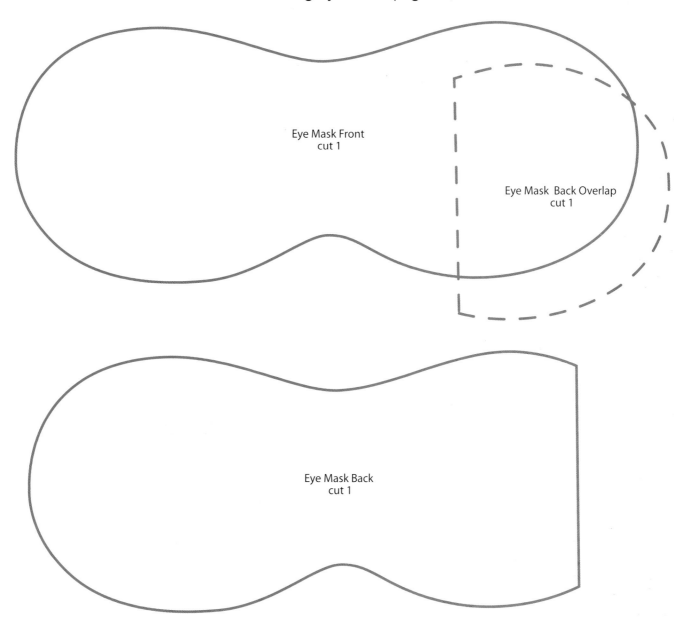

Eye Mask Front
cut 1

Eye Mask Back Overlap
cut 1

Eye Mask Back
cut 1

Patterns

Tag-Along ID Holder (page 77)

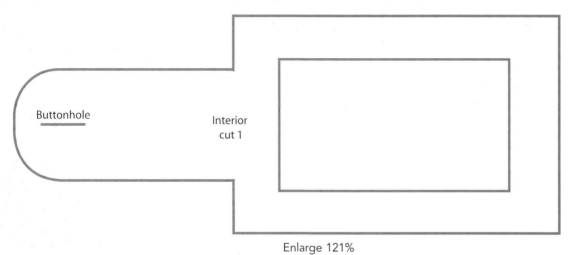

Buttonhole

Interior
cut 1

Enlarge 121%

Acknowledgments

Special thanks go to my mom and grandma for starting me very early on my crafty path; my husband, family and friends for their support and encouragement; and to all my online friends and fans. You all keep me inspired to create every day. Thank you also to my awesome editor Susan Huxley and art director Kathy Holmes, who helped make this book the best it could be.

About the Author

Aimee Ray has been an artist for as long as she can remember. Her mind is always full of ideas, and she loves to try new things. Some of her creative outlets include painting watercolors and creating digital paintings, greeting cards, comic books, and, of course, embroidery.

She is most inspired by nature and animals, dreams, her large collection of books, and other artists. Aimee lives in Northwest Arkansas with her husband and two big, goofy dogs. You can see more of her work at her website, www.dreamfollow.com.

Notes About Suppliers

Usually, the supplies you need for making the projects in Lark books can be found at your local craft supply store, discount mart, home improvement center, or retail shop relevant to the topic of the book. Occasionally, however, you may need to buy materials or tools from specialty suppliers. In order to provide you with the most up-to-date information, we have created a listing of suppliers on our Web site, which we update on a regular basis. Visit us at www.lark-books.com; click on "Craft Supply Sources," and then click on the relevant topic. You will find numerous companies listed with their Web address and/or mailing address and phone number.

Index

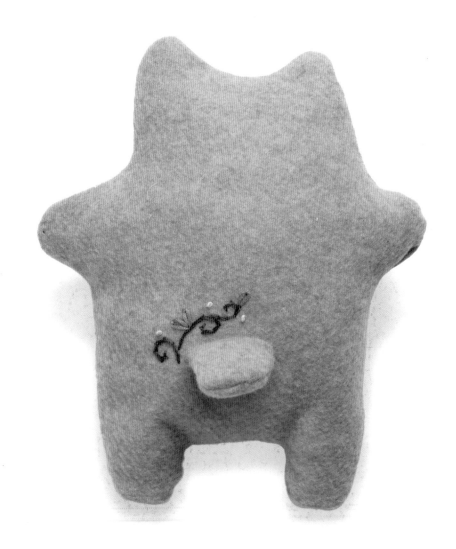